The Witness Stand in Psychological Studies of Crime

Exploring how psychology shapes justice and reveals the hidden forces behind crime

The Witness Stand in Psychological Studies of Crime

Exploring how psychology shapes justice and reveals the hidden forces behind crime

(Illustrated, Refined & Edited)

Hugo Münsterberg

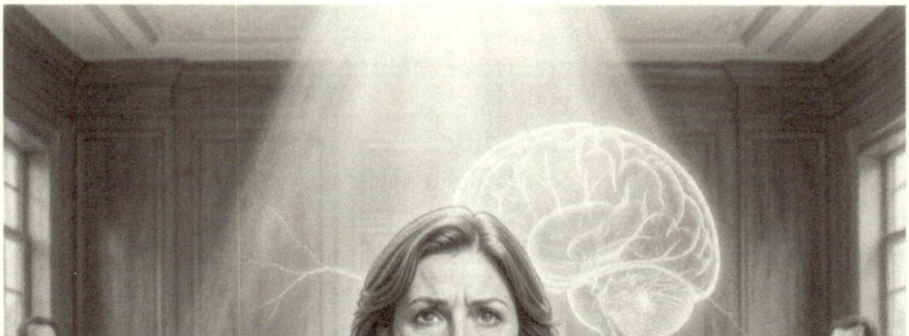

Beyond Books Hub
Books Beyond Imagination

Beyond Books Hub

Books Beyond Imagination

Copyright Notice for Readers

Publication Year: **2026** | Publisher: **Beyond Books**

ISBN: **9789377078485**

Edition: **First Edition, 2026** | Contact: ddsalesglobal@gmail.com

Book Name: **The Witness Stand in Psychological Studies of Crime**

Author: **Hugo Munsterberg**

Price: **Rs 350/-**

Table of Content

Reader's Note

This book is not a casual exploration of crime—it is an invitation to sit inside the human mind at the precise moment when truth, error, and justice collide. *The Witness Stand in Psychological Studies of Crime* challenges one of society's most comfortable assumptions: that what people see, remember, and testify to is reliable. From the very first page, Hugo Münsterberg pulls the reader into a world where certainty dissolves under scientific scrutiny and where justice, as administered by courts, is revealed to be deeply human—and therefore deeply flawed.

What makes this book compelling is not merely its subject matter, but the unsettling clarity with which it exposes the hidden forces shaping legal decisions. Münsterberg does not attack the courtroom from outside; instead, he steps directly into it, illuminating how perception can deceive, memory can distort, and confidence can masquerade as truth. The chapters unfold like a psychological investigation, each one stripping away another layer of assumption that governs trials and verdicts.

The discussion of **illusions of perception** transforms everyday courtroom testimony into a dramatic psychological event. Readers begin to realize that seeing is not believing—and that even honest witnesses can unknowingly present illusions as facts. This realization deepens in the examination of **memory**, where Münsterberg shows that recollection is not a recording but a reconstruction, shaped by emotion, suggestion, and expectation. These insights alone fundamentally change how one listens to any testimony, whether in court or in life.The book's intellectual tension peaks in its exploration of **false confessions**, a topic as tragic as it is urgent. Here, the reader encounters the devastating consequences of psychological pressure, authority, and fear—forces capable of bending innocent minds toward self-destruction. Rather than sensationalizing crime, Münsterberg humanizes it, revealing how psychological vulnerability can turn justice into tragedy.Yet this is not a book of despair. Münsterberg offers a **scientific path forward**, proposing how psychology can serve justice rather than undermine it. From hypnotism's controversial legal role to the foundations of crime prevention, the book balances critique with constructive vision. It suggests that law, when informed by psychological science, can become more humane, accurate, and fair.Readers who value intellectual stimulation will find this work deeply rewarding, but it is equally engaging for those who seek narrative tension and real-world relevance. Every chapter sharpens the reader's awareness—not only of crime and justice, but of the mind itself. By the end, one does not simply finish a book; one emerges changed, more cautious of certainty and more respectful of complexity.This book is for readers who enjoy thinking deeply, questioning authority, and understanding the unseen mechanisms that govern human behavior.

It entertains not by spectacle, but by revelation. Once opened, it becomes impossible to look at a courtroom—or human judgment—the same way again.

Publisher's Note

In presenting *The Witness Stand in Psychological Studies of Crime*, the publisher undertakes a responsibility that goes beyond reproduction—it is a commitment to preservation, clarity, and relevance. Hugo Münsterberg wrote at a time when psychology was only beginning to assert itself as a scientific discipline, yet his insights remain strikingly modern. Our goal in publishing this edition is to ensure that his groundbreaking ideas reach today's readers with the same force, precision, and intellectual honesty that defined the original work.

This book occupies a unique place in the history of both psychology and law. Münsterberg speaks not as a detached theorist, but as a scientist deeply concerned with the real-world consequences of misunderstanding the human mind. His examination of witnesses, confessions, and judicial procedures was radical for its time, and it continues to challenge contemporary assumptions. The publisher has taken great care to preserve the author's original tone—direct, analytical, and occasionally provocative—while ensuring that the language flows smoothly for modern readers. We recognize that readers today approach classic psychological texts with both curiosity and caution. Older works often contain dense arguments or stylistic conventions that can obscure their brilliance. In this edition, clarity has been a guiding principle. Without altering Münsterberg's intent or conclusions, we have ensured that the presentation supports comprehension, allowing readers to focus on ideas rather than struggle with form.

This book is especially relevant in an era where legal systems face increasing scrutiny and psychological evidence plays a growing role in courtrooms worldwide. Münsterberg's insistence that justice must be informed by science rather than intuition aligns strongly with modern concerns about wrongful convictions, coerced confessions, and unreliable testimony.

The publisher believes that revisiting these foundational arguments strengthens public understanding of both law and human behavior.

Above all, this edition is published with respect—for the author, for the reader, and for the seriousness of the subject. We aim to bridge generations of thought, allowing Münsterberg's voice to speak clearly across time. By doing so, we hope to honor his vision: a justice system guided not by appearances, but by knowledge; not by assumption, but by understanding.

This work is offered to students, professionals, and thoughtful readers alike—anyone who believes that truth deserves careful examination and that justice must evolve with insight. We are proud to present this edition as part of our ongoing effort to make enduring intellectual works accessible, engaging, and meaningful in the present age.

Introduction

Today, the United States alone is home to nearly fifty psychological laboratories. Yet, until relatively recently, even well-educated individuals were scarcely aware of their existence. When such laboratories were mentioned, they were often misunderstood. Many imagined them as places devoted to mental healing, telepathy, or spiritistic demonstrations. A common question arose: what possible connection could a laboratory have with the mind? Had the soul not, for nearly two thousand years, belonged to the philosopher? What role, then, could electric batteries, precision instruments, and complex machines play in the study of mental life?

I have encountered these questions many times—unspoken yet unmistakable—on the faces of friends visiting the Psychological Laboratory at Harvard University in Emerson Hall. Their expressions revealed genuine astonishment as they walked through twenty-seven interconnected rooms threaded with electric wires, filled with chronoscopes, kymographs, tachistoscopes, ergographs, and other delicate instruments, while a skilled mechanic worked quietly nearby. To many visitors, such surroundings seemed strangely out of place in any serious inquiry into the mind.

The emergence of this new science escaped widespread attention largely because of the speed of its development. Its growth was so rapid that even its pioneers were surprised by its extent. When I traveled as a young student to the University of Leipzig in the early 1880s, the small psychological laboratory founded by Professor Wilhelm Wundt was still the only one of its kind in the world. No university of standing today would consider itself adequately equipped with the modest rooms in which the master and his small group of students once carried out their experiments. Yet from those humble beginnings, the Leipzig laboratory expanded steadily. Each passing year saw the founding of new institutes—first by Wundt's direct pupils and later by their students in turn.

The first German laboratory outside Leipzig was the one I established at Freiburg nearly twenty years ago. Around the same time, Stanley Hall and James McKeen Cattell carried the work from Leipzig across the Atlantic. Today, it is difficult to find a university of recognized standing that has not established a workshop dedicated to this youngest of the natural sciences.

Even more striking than this outward expansion has been the inner growth of psychology itself. If the science began in modest surroundings, its original ambitions were even more restrained. Experimental psychology did not initially create its own problems; instead, it borrowed them from neighboring sciences. Physiologists and physicians were already conducting careful investigations into the functions of the eye, ear, skin, and muscles. In doing so, they obtained—often unintentionally—results of deep psychological significance concerning seeing, hearing, touching, and acting. Physicists, concerned with the limits of human perception as a means of understanding the external world, produced findings that directly illuminated the psychology of perception. Astronomers, troubled by what they called the "personal equation," discovered that different observers required different amounts of time to register the same celestial event.

In attempting to solve this problem, they measured the speed with which impressions are noticed and acted upon, an inquiry that led directly into the core of mental life.

Thus, scientists who had little direct interest in psychology accumulated a rich body of experimental findings with clear psychological meaning. Psychologists could no longer afford to overlook these results. It was no longer defensible to claim, for instance, that thought is instantaneous when astronomical observations had shown that even the simplest mental act requires measurable time. Experimental psychology therefore began by repeating, from its own standpoint, investigations that others had undertaken for entirely different purposes.

At first, it appeared that such work would yield only marginal insights—facts lying at the boundary between mind and body. Few imagined that experimental methods could ever be applied to the higher realms of inner life, which seemed to belong solely to the philosopher. Yet once psychology secured its own laboratories, it became natural to extend the experimental method to new and increasingly broader domains.

Research soon turned toward memory and the association of ideas, then toward attention and imagination, spatial perception, and the sense of time.

Gradually, experimental inquiry was applied to feeling and emotion, impulse and will, imitation and reasoning. Mental functions that only a short time earlier appeared beyond the reach of laboratory study now proved open to systematic investigation. Today, there is scarcely any aspect of mental life into which experimental psychology has not directed its illuminating searchlight.

It may appear surprising that a development of such significance progressed for so long in apparent isolation from everyday life. Perception and memory, feeling and emotion, attention and will—these are not abstract curiosities but the very forces that shape our work, our pleasures, our responsibilities, and our professions. And yet, for many years, no clear road led from the calm seclusion of the psychological laboratory to the noisy, urgent world of practical affairs.

This separation, however, was not a weakness in the growth of psychology. A science gains little by turning prematurely toward application. The longer a discipline matures under the sole discipline of truth-seeking, the stronger and more reliable its foundations become. Experimental psychology has now reached a stage of development at which it is both natural and justified to consider how it may serve the practical needs of life.

This intention must not be misunderstood. To make psychology useful does not mean to tear fragments of theory from their context and present them crudely to the public. Such misguided efforts have been attempted too often, and their consequences have been unfortunate. Half-digested psychological ideas have been imposed upon schoolteachers, while educational conferences have been burdened with diagrams of ganglion cells and tables of reaction times that enlighten no one. No warning against this form of superficial or sensational "yellow psychology" can be stated too strongly.

If experimental psychology is to enter a genuine period of practical service, research itself must be reshaped so that it confronts practical problems directly. When questions of education are involved, psychological experiments must begin with educational realities. Applied psychology must therefore develop as an independent experimental science, related to pure experimental psychology in the same way that engineering stands in relation to physics.

The moment for such applied work is clearly approaching, and progress is already visible in many directions. The principal fields of application may be broadly identified as education, medicine, art, economics, and law. Educators readily recognize that systematic investigations of memory, attention, and learning can provide firm guidance for teaching. Physicians increasingly acknowledge that psychological research deepens our understanding of nervous and mental disorders, pain, and the mental factors involved in healing. Artists may discover that their intuitive creativity is enriched—not restricted—by psychological studies of color, form, rhythm, harmony, suggestion, and aesthetic feeling. The world of business, too, is beginning to realize that economic efficiency depends in countless ways on psychological conditions: the organization of labor, the power of advertising to attract attention, and the qualities that make salesmanship effective.

Politicians who seek to shape public opinion, scientists engaged in discovery, military officers responsible for discipline, and ministers striving to inspire minds all increasingly sense that applied psychology can offer them genuine assistance. The lawyer alone remains largely resistant. Judges, jurors, and attorneys are often convinced that legal instinct and common sense are sufficient, and they fail to recognize that experimental psychology—guided by the work of Binet, Stern, Lipmann, Jung, Wertheimer, Gross, Sommer, Aschaffenburg, and others—has already made substantial progress in this field. If psychology is ever to assume its rightful place in the administration of justice, this will not occur through technical treatises alone, but through clear and accessible discussion addressed to the broader public, whose informed judgment may ultimately exert the pressure necessary for reform.

With this purpose in mind, and while engaged in preparing a comprehensive and technically precise treatise on applied psychology, I have written the following more popular sketches. They do not attempt to be exhaustive; they are selective, and they focus only on a few problems at the point where psychology and law directly meet. These chapters are concerned primarily with the mental life of the witness on the witness stand. Only the final section, which addresses the prevention of crime, departs from this central theme. I have not yet undertaken a discussion of the psychology of the attorney, the judge, or the jury—subjects that are particularly well suited to experimental investigation. Even the psychology of the witness is treated here only in outline. My sole aim is to draw the attention of thoughtful and responsible readers to a field that has been astonishingly neglected, yet one that urgently demands the serious consideration of the social community.

Chapter–1. Illusions of Perception in The Courtroom

In every courtroom, people swear to tell the truth—yet their stories often sharply disagree. How can honest witnesses see the same event so differently? This chapter uncovers the hidden limits of human perception and shows how memory, attention, expectation, and suggestion shape what we believe we see and hear.

There was an automobile accident. Before the court, one witness, having sworn to tell "the whole truth and nothing but the truth," testified that the road was entirely dry and covered with dust. Another witness, speaking with equal confidence, declared that it had rained and that the road was muddy. One insisted that the automobile was moving very slowly; the other maintained that he had never seen a vehicle traveling at such speed. The first stated that only two or three people were present on the village road; the second was certain that many men, women, and children were passing by. Both witnesses were respectable citizens, neither of whom had the slightest motive to distort the facts as they honestly remembered them. Among my notes I find another case in which everything depended on the interval between a whistle heard from the street and the sound of an explosion.

It was of decisive importance for the court to determine whether this interval was long enough to allow a person to walk a certain distance—an action requiring at least half a minute Of two impartial witnesses, one swore that the time was less than ten seconds; the other declared, with equal certainty, that it exceeded a full minute.

In another instance, it was essential to establish whether, during a disturbance, the number of guests in a hall exceeded the forty who had been invited. Some witnesses insisted that no more than twenty people could have been present, while others were convinced that they had seen more than one hundred. In a poisoning case, several members of the family testified that the beverage had a sour and unpleasant taste; others claimed it was tasteless; still others asserted that it was sweet. In a street brawl, one witness was convinced that a man had seized a beer mug and struck his companion's skull with it, holding it firmly in his hand. Others stated with equal certainty that the two men were separated by a long table and that the mug had been thrown as a missile from a distance of six or eight feet.

In another trial, one witness observed, by moonlight at the seashore, a woman carrying a child; another was no less certain that it was a man walking with a dog. More recently, passengers on a train passing a courtyard testified under oath that they had caught, at a glance, the scene of a man whipping a child. One described him as clean-shaven, wearing a hat, and standing; another was equally sure that he had a full beard, wore no hat, and was seated on a bench. On yet another occasion, two highly reliable expert stenographers were convinced that they had accurately recorded the spoken words they heard, and yet their transcripts differed widely on matters of real importance.

There is no need to multiply such examples drawn from actual cases. Anyone who recalls the major criminal trials of recent years knows how regularly such contradictions among witnesses arise. Let us, however, set aside all situations that require technical or professional knowledge.

Our concern here is limited to direct observations and impressions that demand no special expertise. Wherever specialized knowledge is required, differences of opinion are to be expected, and one conscientious expert may honestly contradict another. Nor are we concerned with deliberate falsehood. The witness who lies offers little psychological interest for the study of illusion. Questions of mental disease are likewise excluded. What remains are the unintentional errors of the healthy mind. At this point, the psychologist must ask a decisive question: are all these errors of the same nature? Is it sufficient to dismiss them merely as illusions of memory?

It is customary to place the burden of error entirely upon memory. It is generally assumed that perception itself is uniform and trustworthy. If there were only twenty people in a hall, it is argued, no one could possibly have perceived one hundred. If the road was muddy, no one could have seen it as dusty. If the man was clean-shaven, no one could have seen a beard. Any disagreement, therefore, must have arisen later, through the distortions of recollection. Perception is assumed to be correct; reproduction faulty.

But is this assumption justified? Do we all truly perceive the same situation in the same way, and does it carry the same meaning for each of us at the very moment of experience? Is the court sufficiently aware of the profound differences in human perception? Does it adequately examine the capacities, habits, and modes of attention through which a witness moves in the world he believes he observes?

Certainly, a certain amount of what is called common sense has always entered, consciously or unconsciously, into judicial decisions. Contradictory testimony must be weighed, and judges have often felt compelled to philosophize or psychologize on their own account. Yet consultation with psychological authorities was long regarded as unnecessary, even improper. Legal theory has sometimes taken pride in the belief that judges have always found their way without psychological guidance. And yet the records of many cases—particularly those involving railroad accidents and claims for damages—show that the psychological intuitions of the bench have often stood in direct contradiction to demonstrable facts.

A judge may seek to reinforce a decision by citing precedents, but even if an earlier ruling was justified, is the untrained psychologist on the bench truly equipped to decide whether the mental situation in a new case is genuinely the same? Such judicial self-reliance may have been unavoidable at a time when psychology itself was vague and speculative. That situation, however, has changed fundamentally. With the emergence of exact and experimental psychology, the continued neglect of psychological insight in legal judgment can no longer be defended.

The study of these mental processes no longer lies outside the domain of science. In light of the progress of experimental psychology, it is an evident incongruity that the State should devote its greatest efforts to clarifying every physical detail of an event, yet never call upon the psychological expert to assess the factor that often proves most decisive—the mind of the witness. From time to time, the demand has been raised that the memory of the witness be tested by the methods of modern psychology. It must be added, however, that the study of perceptive judgment itself must also find its way into the courtroom.

Last winter, almost incidentally, I conducted a small experiment with the students of my regular psychology course at Harvard. Several hundred young men, mostly between twenty and twenty-three years of age, took part. The test was of the simplest kind. Without any theoretical introduction, at the beginning of an ordinary lecture, I asked them to write careful answers to a number of questions concerning what they would see or hear. I urged them to respond as conscientiously and accurately as possible. The hundreds of answers I received clearly showed that each participant had done his best. For the present purpose, I shall confine my report to the first hundred papers selected at random.

I first showed them a large sheet of white cardboard on which fifty small black squares were pasted in irregular order. I exposed it for five seconds and then asked how many black spots were on the sheet. The answers ranged from twenty-five to two hundred. Estimates above one hundred were more frequent than those below fifty. Only three students felt unable to give a definite answer. I then showed a second cardboard containing only twenty such spots. This time the estimates ranged from ten to seventy. Here we had highly trained, attentive observers, whose attention was fully focused and who had ample time for quiet inspection. Yet in both cases some believed they had seen seven or eight times as many points as others. And still, we are inclined to doubt the sincerity of two courtroom witnesses when one is convinced that he saw two hundred people in a hall where another found only twenty-five.

My next inquiry concerned the perception of time. I asked the students to estimate how many seconds passed between two loud clicks. In the first test, the interval between the clicks was ten seconds; in a second experiment, it was three seconds. When the actual interval was ten seconds, the estimates ranged from half a second to sixty seconds, with a considerable number judging forty-five seconds to be correct. The one student who called it half a second was Chinese, while all those whose judgments ranged from one second to sixty seconds were average Americans. When the objective interval was three seconds, the estimates varied between half a second and fifteen seconds. I emphasize that these wide fluctuations appeared despite the fact that the students knew in advance that they were to estimate a time interval. The variation would almost certainly have been greater had the question been asked afterward, without prior warning. And yet a district attorney confidently expects a reliable answer when he asks a witness—perhaps a cab driver—how much time elapsed between a cry and a gunshot.

In my third experiment, I sought to examine how rapidity is perceived. On the platform stood a large clock with a white dial, over which a single black pointer completed one full revolution in five seconds. The arrow-shaped tip of the pointer moved along the edge of the dial at a speed of ten centimeters per second—that is, in one second it traveled roughly the length of a finger. I allowed the clock to run for a full minute and asked the observers to watch carefully and then describe, either numerically or by comparison with familiar moving objects, the speed at which the pointer moved.

Most preferred comparisons. The descriptions included: a man walking slowly; a local train; a bicyclist; a funeral procession in a city street; a trotting dog; faster than a man's trot; an electric streetcar; an express train; a goldfish in water; the fastest automobile speed; very slow, like a snail; a lively spider; and many others. Is it conceivable that university students, trained in observation, could watch a movement continuously for a full minute and yet disagree so completely—some judging it slower than a snail, others faster than an express train? And yet the design of the experiment excluded every possible error of memory and eliminated suggestion. The observation was deliberate, calm, and unhurried.

Those who expressed their judgments in numerical terms showed no less variation. The estimates included: one revolution in two seconds; one revolution in forty-five seconds; three inches per second; twelve feet per second; thirty seconds per hundred yards; seven miles per hour; fifteen miles per hour; forty miles per hour; and so forth. In reality, the pointer would have traveled only about one-third of a mile in an hour. Many of the estimates, therefore, exaggerated the true speed by more than one hundred times.

In my next test, I asked the class to describe a sound they would hear and to identify its source. The sound was produced by striking a large tuning fork with a small hammer beneath the desk, out of sight of the students. Among the hundred papers examined for this record, exactly two recognized the sound as that of a tuning fork.

All others identified it as a bell, an organ pipe, a muffled gong, a brass instrument, a horn, a cello string, a violin, and the like. Some compared it to sounds as diverse as a lion's growl, a steam whistle, a foghorn, a flywheel, or a human voice.

The descriptions of the sound were equally diverse: soft, mellow, humming, deep, dull, solemn, resonant, penetrating, full, rumbling, clear, low—but also rough, sharp, and whistling. Once again, it must be emphasized that everyone knew beforehand that he was to observe the sound, which was announced by a signal. How much greater would the divergence have been had the sound occurred unexpectedly—a tone that even now appeared soft to some and harsh to others, like a bell to one observer and a whistle to the next.

I then turned to a series of experiments involving visual interpretation. I showed several sheets of white cardboard, each containing a variety of dark and light ink spots arranged in a somewhat fanciful pattern. Each card was displayed for two seconds, and it was suggested that these rough ink drawings represented something in the external world. Immediately after viewing a card, the students were asked to write down what the drawing represented.

In some cases, the observers remained skeptical and stated that the spots represented nothing at all, merely random ink blots. In the majority of cases, however, the suggestion was effective, and a definite object was perceived. The list of interpretations for one picture included: soldiers in a valley; grapes; a palace; a riverbank; a Japanese landscape; foliage; a rabbit; a woodland scene; a town with towers; a rising storm; the shore of a lake; a garden; flags; figures in a landscape; hair in curling papers; a china plate; a war scene; a village square; a lake in a jungle; trees with a stone wall; clouds; a harvest scene; an elephant; a map; a lake with a castle in the background; trees; and many others.

For the next picture, which contained finer details, the responses included: a spider; a landscape; a turtle; a butterfly; a woman's head; a cluster of war flags; ballet dancers; a crowd of people; a cactus plant; a skunk walking along a log; a centipede; a boat on a pond; a crow's nest; a beetle; a flower; an island; and so on. With the exception of the vague term "landscape," repetitions were rare.

We have known since the days of Hamlet and Polonius that a cloud may resemble a camel or a whale. Yet the sheer richness and diversity of these interpretations could scarcely have been anticipated. They reveal, with striking clarity, how deeply individual perception shapes what we believe we see, hear, and understand.

My next question did not concern immediate perception, but rather a memory image so vivid and familiar to everyone that I felt justified in using it as a substitute for direct perception. I asked the students to compare the apparent size of the full moon with that of some object held in the hand at arm's length. I explained carefully that they were to imagine an object just large enough, when held at arm's length, to cover the entire disc of the full moon.

The list of answers began as follows: a quarter of a dollar; a fair-sized cantaloupe; at the horizon, a large dinner plate, overhead, a dessert plate; my watch; six inches in diameter; a silver dollar; a hundred times as large as my watch; a man's head; a fifty-cent piece; nine inches in diameter; a grapefruit; a carriage wheel; a butter plate; an orange; ten feet; two inches; a one-cent piece; a classroom clock; a pea; a soup plate; a fountain pen; a lemon pie; the palm of the hand; three feet in diameter. The diversity of these answers once again reveals the overwhelming multiplicity of impressions received from what seems to be a single, familiar object.

To the surprise of many readers, it must be stated at once that only one student gave the correct answer: the one who compared the moon to a pea. It is highly unlikely that the results would have been different had I asked the same question on a clear night with the full moon directly overhead.

The substitution of a memory image for immediate perception can hardly have impaired the accuracy of the judgment. If, in any court of law, witnesses were asked to estimate the size of a distant object, and one declared that it appeared no larger than a pea at arm's length, another as large as a lemon pie, and a third as ten feet in diameter, it would hardly be fair to reach an objective conclusion before a psychologist had examined the mental factors influencing those estimates.

There were many additional experiments, but in order to avoid technical detail I shall refer to only two more, which are closely related. First, I showed the students several pairs of colored paper squares and allowed them ample time to write down which of the two appeared darker. The first pair consisted of red and blue, the second of blue and green, and the third of blue and gray. My chief interest lay in the last pair. The gray was objectively much lighter than the dark blue, and any unbiased observer, looking carefully at the two squares, could hardly doubt that the blue was darker. Yet approximately one-fifth of the students wrote that the gray appeared darker.

This result should be kept in mind when considering the final experiment I wish to describe. I stood on the platform behind a low desk and asked the students to watch closely and describe everything I would do between two given signals. At the first signal, I lifted with my right hand a small rotating wheel with a color disc, set it in motion so that its colors changed, and held it at the level of my head, while keeping my gaze fixed eagerly upon it.

At the same time, and continuing until the final signal, I performed a series of actions with my left hand: first, I took a pencil from my vest pocket and wrote something on the desk; then I removed my watch and placed it on the table; next, I took a silver cigarette case from my pocket, opened it, removed a cigarette, closed the case with a loud click, and returned it to my pocket. Then the closing signal was given.

The results were striking. Eighteen out of the hundred students reported that they had noticed nothing at all of what I did with my left hand. Pencil, watch, and cigarette case had simply not existed for them.

The fact that I myself appeared to direct all my attention to the color wheel had evidently inhibited their perception of the other actions. This occurred despite the fact that my movements with the left hand were deliberately conspicuous and that I had previously emphasized the importance of observing every single action. The outcome demonstrated how readily attention, once narrowly directed, can render us blind to everything else.

In this respect, the famous medium who claimed that once she had drawn a client's attention to the slate in her hand he would not notice an elephant passing behind her through the room may have been closer to the truth than we like to admit.

The most remarkable fact, however, lay elsewhere. Of those eighteen students who failed to notice the actions of my left hand, fourteen were the same individuals who, in the earlier experiment, judged the light gray square to be darker than the dark blue. This coincidence was certainly not accidental. In the color experiment, the mere idea of grayness had led their suggestible minds to assume that a colorless gray must be darker than any color. Their judgment was not guided by optical impression at all, but entirely by an abstract conception. The coincidence therefore demonstrated how quickly a simple experiment, using nothing more than two pieces of colored paper, can identify individuals who may be unreliable reporters of events occurring before their eyes. Whatever they expect to see, they do see; and when their attention is directed in one direction, they become blind, deaf, and helpless in another.

Enough has been said of classroom experiments. Yet do they not serve as a serious warning against blind confidence in the observations of the average, healthy individual? Do they not strengthen the demand for a more careful study of individual differences among those who appear on the witness stand? Such a study, however, would be incomplete if the psychologist were concerned only with differences between individuals, with showing how one person's observation may diverge radically from another's.

The psychologist in the courtroom must give equal attention to those illusions that are common to all human beings and of which ordinary common sense remains largely ignorant.

Jurors and judges do not usually question whether a witness who claims to have seen a woman in a red dress at twilight might have been mistaken for one in blue. They are not expected to know that under faint illumination blue sensations may still arise while red sensations have already vanished. They are rarely aware of how directions of sound are confused by everyone, or that while we may easily distinguish whether a cry comes from the right or the left, we may be utterly unable to decide whether it came from in front or from behind. They may not know that the victim of a crime could be completely unable to perceive that he was stabbed with a sharp instrument, experiencing the sensation instead as a dull blow. Witnesses testify about the taste of poisoned liquids, and yet few in the jury box are aware that the same substance can taste quite differently on different parts of the tongue.

In civil cases, disputing parties describe the size, length, and shape of a field as it appeared to them, without anyone reminding the court that the same distance can appear entirely different under countless varying conditions.

A judge listens to a description of events secretly observed through a keyhole, without understanding why judgments of size and position are almost certainly distorted under such circumstances.

A witness may be convinced that he felt something wet, when in fact he touched nothing more than smooth, cold metal. In short, every chapter of sensory psychology offers tools for reducing the confusion and chaos that dominate eyewitness observation.

And yet perception alone is never the whole story. Associations, judgments, and suggestions penetrate every act of observation. We know from children's drawings that they depict not only what they see, but what they know exists. In much the same way, adults believe they perceive at least what they expect to find.

I recall experiments in my laboratory in which printed words were exposed for an instant under sudden illumination. Whenever I spoke a sentence beforehand, I could influence what the subject believed he saw. When the printed word was *courage,* and I spoke about university life, the subject read *college*. When the word was *Philistines,* and I casually mentioned colonial policy, it was read as *Philippines*. In precisely this way, misleading advertisements cause us to overlook critical details that entirely change the meaning of an offer.

Experimental psychology has at last cleared the ground. To ignore this science and to rely solely on the primitive psychology of common sense is no longer defensible when crime and punishment are at stake and when an analysis of the witness's mind may alter the entire outcome of a case.

It is enough that we must endure these mental limitations in everyday life; the courtroom, at least, should strive to come closer to the truth and to set an example.

Other institutions may then follow in time. Perhaps even newspapers will one day learn from legal practice and examine the observational capacity of their witnesses as well.

After discovering that my own students cannot agree on whether a point moves as slowly as a snail or as rapidly as an express train; whether a time interval lasts half a second or a full minute; whether there are twenty-five points or two hundred; whether a sound comes from a whistle, a gong, or a violin; whether the moon is as small as a pea or as large as a man, I am no longer surprised by contradictions in newspaper reports.

Not long ago, I delivered a lecture on peace in New York before a large audience, followed by an unexpected and spirited response.

Reporters were seated directly in front of the platform. One wrote that the audience was so astonished by my speech that it listened in complete silence; another reported that I was repeatedly interrupted by loud applause and that the applause continued for several minutes at the end.

One stated that during my opponent's remarks I smiled constantly; another insisted that my face remained gray and expressionless. One described me as turning purple-red with excitement; another claimed I grew white as chalk. One reported that my critic paced back and forth across the stage; another that he stood beside me the entire time, patting me in a fatherly manner on the shoulder. And finally, Mr. Dooley heard that before speaking on peace I had been introduced as a professor from the Harvard War School—though it may be that Mr. Dooley himself was not present.

Chapter of the End

Chapter–2.
The Fallibility of The Witness's Memory

Memory feels strong and certain, especially under oath. But is it truly reliable? This chapter shows how even honest and intelligent people can remember events incorrectly—adding, changing, or forgetting details without knowing it.

Last summer I found myself standing before a jury, not as an expert, but as a witness. While my family and I were spending time at the seashore, my house in the city had been burglarized. The police apprehended a suspect in possession of part of the stolen property, and I was summoned to testify about what I had observed and discovered.

Under oath, I reported that the burglars had entered through a cellar window and described the rooms they had visited. To establish that the crime had occurred at night, I stated that I had found drops of candle wax on the second floor. To show that the intruders intended to return, I testified that they had left a large mantel clock, carefully packed in wrapping paper, on the dining-room table. Finally, when asked about the amount of clothing taken, I asserted that the burglars had not removed more than the specific list of items I had already provided to the police.

Only a few days later, I discovered that every one of these statements was incorrect. The burglars had not entered through a window at all, but had forced the lock of the cellar door. The clock had not been wrapped in paper, but in a tablecloth. The candle drippings were not on the second floor, but in the attic. The list of stolen garments had to be expanded by seven additional pieces. And while my sworn testimony repeatedly referred to two burglars, I could not be certain that more than one person had been involved.

How did all these errors arise? I cannot excuse myself by claiming a weak memory. Over the past eighteen years, I have delivered approximately three thousand university lectures. For those thousands of coherent addresses, I never relied on written notes or outlines, and I have never once been forced to pause in search of a name or a line of thought. My memory, therefore, has served me generously. Nor was I prejudiced against the defendant. Since he could reasonably expect to spend the next twelve years in circumstances that would afford him little opportunity to read my writings, I may frankly admit that I felt no personal animosity toward him. I stood before the court under conditions most favorable to telling the whole truth and nothing but the truth. Yet, to my own alarm, I discovered how many illusions had entered my testimony.

The explanation is not difficult to trace. I had not conducted a careful or systematic examination of the house. As soon as the police informed me of the burglary, I rushed back from the seashore, anxious that valuable contents might have been destroyed or stolen. When I realized that the intruders had treated me rather mildly—having begun in the wine cellar and apparently forgotten, under its generous influence, the greater purpose of their visit—I made only a superficial inspection. The image of the clock lying on the table, packed and ready to be taken away, impressed itself vividly upon my mind. But the fact that it was wrapped in a tablecloth made too faint an impression to survive. My imagination gradually replaced this detail with the more familiar image of wrapping paper, and I was prepared to swear to it until I returned at the end of the summer and saw the facts again.

In the same way, I retained a clear image of candle drippings on the floor. But since, at the moment of perception, no special importance attached to the exact location, my memory slowly substituted the second floor for the attic. I knew with certainty, from scattered papers and other signs of disorder, that both places had been ransacked, and this knowledge silently reshaped my recollection.

As for the missing clothes, I had simply forgotten that I had stored several suits in a distant wardrobe. Only later did I discover that it, too, had been emptied.

My remaining errors arose clearly from the power of suggestion. From the very beginning, the police and everyone around the house assumed that entry had been gained through a cellar window, since forcing the locked doors seemed more difficult. I never seriously examined the alternative, although it was later discovered that the burglars had succeeded in removing the lock from a door. Finally, my sworn account consistently referred to two burglars, without the slightest doubt at the time. In fact, the man they arrested had been caught a few days later while robbing another house. He shot a policeman during his arrest, and in his room they found a jacket bearing my name, sewn in by the tailor. That discovery alone suggested that my house had also been burglarized.

From the very start, however, the man insisted that he had acted with an accomplice and that the other had taken the remaining stolen goods.

The supposed accomplice was never found and may still be wearing my cufflinks. Yet I never heard any serious doubt raised about his existence.

Through mere imitation of this assumption, I myself never questioned the presence of a second burglar, despite the fact that every aspect of the crime could just as easily have been carried out by one person alone. After all, a man capable of stealing and shooting might also be capable of lying.

Thus, despite the best intentions, a reliable memory, and a calm state of mind, my sworn testimony contained a complex mixture of confusion, illusion, forgetting, faulty inference, and submission to suggestion.

My only consolation lies in the fact that in thousands of courtrooms across the world, witnesses every day swear to far more serious combinations of truth and error—blends of memory and illusion, knowledge and suggestion, experience and mistaken conclusion.

In my own case, none of these errors had serious consequences. But is it reasonable to assume that this is always so? Is it not far more likely that every day, errors enter the machinery of justice through testimony that bears all the outward marks of honesty and reliability? Judges, juries, and later the readers of newspapers do their best to weigh the evidence.

Not every sworn statement is accepted as absolute truth, and contradictions between witnesses are well known. Yet instinctive doubt usually focuses on veracity.

The public tends to suspect that a witness lies, while assuming that a normal, responsible person may forget something but could not possibly remember it incorrectly.

Confidence in the reliability of memory is so widespread that suspicion of memory illusion plays only a minor role in the mind of the juror.

Even the cross-examining lawyer is usually governed by the belief that a false statement must be the result of deliberate deception. This belief, however, is itself a popular illusion—one against which modern psychology must firmly protest.

Justice would fail less often if those who evaluate evidence were more aware of the treacherous nature of human memory. It is striking that courts employ the most refined scientific methods when, for example, a drop of dried blood must be examined in a murder case, yet remain content with crude intuition and common prejudice when evaluating a mental product such as a witness's memory. No juror would be expected to rely on general impressions when deciding whether a bloodstain is human or animal. Yet the same juror is expected to determine whether a witness's memories are faithful reproductions of past experience or distorted by association and suggestion.

The court proceeds as if physiological chemistry had advanced to remarkable precision, while experimental psychology—the science devoted to analyzing mental processes—had remained unchanged since antiquity. Such an attitude is no longer defensible. When liberty and justice are at stake, the scientific study of memory deserves the same respect as the scientific analysis of blood.

The fact is that experimental psychology has not only made remarkable progress during recent decades, but has also devoted, especially in recent years, an exceptional degree of attention to precisely those problems that arise on the witness stand. It is hardly an exaggeration to say that a new and specialized field of study has emerged, devoted exclusively to the reliability of memory. This movement began in Germany and for several years even maintained a journal of its own. At the same time, research in France and the United States developed along similar lines, and the work quickly spread throughout psychological laboratories across the world.

A vast body of valuable material has been gathered. Yet practical jurisprudence remains, for the most part, unaware of it. While the alienist is always a welcome figure in the courtroom, the psychologist is still regarded as an outsider. Courts will readily devote days to listening to the so-called science of handwriting experts, yet hesitate to permit an examination of a witness with regard to memory, perception, attention, association, volition, and suggestibility—examined by methods grounded in the exact standards of experimental psychology. It is far easier to be satisfied with sharp, reassuring divisions: a person is sane or insane; if sane, he tells the truth or he lies. The psychologist, by his very presence, would disturb this comfortable simplicity.

The practice of administering an oath contributes significantly to this mistaken valuation of evidence. Its solemnity and seriousness suggest that, once a witness resolves not to lie, the conditions for complete truth are fully secured. We are too ready to confuse truth in a subjective sense with truth in an objective sense. A German proverb says, "Children and fools speak the truth," and alongside it stands the saying, "In vino veritas." No one seriously believes that children, fools, or intoxicated individuals possess deeper insight into reality than sober, rational adults. What is meant is simply that the motives which often lead to the intentional suppression of truth are absent. Children do not conceal the truth because they are naïve; fools do not conceal it because they are reckless; and intoxicated minds do not conceal it because the inhibiting mechanisms of self-control are temporarily weakened. Subjective truthfulness may thus be present, while the content of speech remains objectively false from beginning to end.

It is only in this limited sense that the oath, through its religious background and its association with punishment, can promote truth. It can substantially reduce the intention to deceive. Whether it can increase objective accuracy to the same degree is an entirely different question.

It is well known that the oath exerts another influence as well. It does not merely suppress intentional falsehood; it also sharpens attention. It discourages careless or casual recollection and calls forth deliberate mental effort. The witness feels a moral obligation to apply his full will in reproducing the whole truth and nothing but the truth.

No psychologist would deny this effect. The question is whether intention alone is sufficient, and whether increased attention necessarily improves memory in all respects.

Our mental functions do not always perform best under intense scrutiny. We may speak fluently until we begin to focus deliberately on the movements of our lips and tongue; once we do so, speech often becomes awkward and inhibited. Is it certain that memory functions flawlessly simply because we urgently wish it to do so? We may strain to recall a name and fail entirely, only to find that it returns effortlessly after our attention has been diverted elsewhere. Is it not possible that the determined effort to recall accurately under oath may be far less effective than public opinion assumes? A strong subjective feeling of certainty is no guarantee of objective truth.

Several years ago, a striking experiment was conducted in Berlin at the university seminar of Professor von Liszt, the well-known criminologist. During a lecture, the professor referred to a book. Suddenly, one of the older students exclaimed, "I wish to discuss the matter from the standpoint of Christian morality!" Another student retorted sharply, "I cannot tolerate that!" The first sprang up, shouting, "You have insulted me!" The second clenched his fist and cried, "If you say another word—!" The first drew a revolver. The second rushed toward him. The professor stepped between them, and as he seized the man's arm, the revolver discharged. Chaos erupted.

At that moment, Professor von Liszt restored order and asked some of the students to write a precise account of what had occurred. The entire episode, it later emerged, was a carefully planned and rehearsed performance by the three participants, designed specifically to test the accuracy of observation and recollection. Some students wrote their reports immediately; others were asked to write theirs the following day or even a week later; still others gave their accounts under cross-examination.

The objective sequence of events was divided into fourteen distinct elements, involving both actions and spoken words. Errors were counted as omissions, additions, or alterations.

Even the most accurate report contained errors amounting to twenty-six percent; the most inaccurate reached eighty percent. Reports concerning the second half of the incident, which was more emotionally charged, contained on average fifteen percent more errors than those describing the first half. Words were attributed to individuals who had remained silent throughout; actions were ascribed to participants for which no trace existed; and essential elements of the staged drama vanished entirely from the memory of many witnesses.

These findings speak with unmistakable clarity. They demonstrate that even under conditions of sincerity, attention, and emotional engagement, memory remains vulnerable to distortion. And they show, beyond doubt, that justice can no longer afford to rely solely on intuition and common sense when evaluating the testimony of witnesses.

This striking psychological experiment, conducted six years ago, gave rise to a long series of similar investigations carried out in many different places, each seeking to refine and improve the experimental conditions.

One requirement, however, always remained essential: the complete naïveté of the witnesses. The slightest suspicion that an experiment was taking place would have destroyed its value. Indeed, it was considered desirable that even the writing of the report should be done while the participants still believed the event to be real.

Two years ago, for example, such an experiment was conducted in Göttingen during a meeting of a scientific association composed of jurists, psychologists, and physicians—individuals, therefore, trained in careful observation. On the same evening, a public carnival celebration was taking place somewhere on the same street. Suddenly, in the midst of the scholarly meeting, the doors burst open. A clown in a brightly colored costume rushed into the room in apparent panic, followed closely by a Black man holding a revolver. In the center of the hall, first one and then the other shouted excited phrases; then one fell to the ground, the other jumped upon him; a shot rang out, and suddenly both men disappeared. The entire scene lasted less than twenty seconds.

Everyone present was completely taken by surprise. With the exception of the presiding officer, no one had the slightest idea that every word and action had been carefully rehearsed in advance, or that photographs had been taken to record the scene. It seemed entirely natural, therefore, when the president asked the members to write down, individually and in detail, an exact account of what had happened, explaining that the matter might well come before the courts.

Of the forty reports submitted, only one contained omissions amounting to less than twenty percent of the characteristic actions. Fourteen omitted between twenty and forty percent of the essential facts; twelve omitted between forty and fifty percent; and thirteen omitted more than fifty percent. Beyond these omissions, only six of the forty reports were free from positively false statements. In twenty-four reports, up to ten percent of the statements were pure inventions, and in ten reports—fully one quarter of the total—more than ten percent of the statements were entirely false. This occurred despite the fact that all observers were scientifically trained.

Only four out of the forty noticed that the man with the revolver wore nothing on his head. All others invented headgear for him: a derby hat, a top hat, and various other forms. In addition, observers described him as wearing a red suit, a brown suit, a striped suit, a coffee-colored jacket, shirt sleeves, and similar garments. In reality, he wore white trousers and a black jacket with a large red necktie. The scientific commission that analyzed the results concluded that the majority of observers either omitted or falsified approximately half of the events that had occurred directly before their eyes. As might be expected, estimates of the duration of the incident varied widely, ranging from a few seconds to several minutes.

There is no need to multiply accounts of these dramatic experiments, which have recently become so popular that they are almost treated as a form of sport. They will, however, need to be continued under a wide variety of conditions if the psychological laws involved are to be fully understood. At present, several points remain unsettled. Some experiments suggest that errors made after a week are scarcely more frequent than those made after a single day. Other studies indicate that the number of errors steadily increases with the passage of time. Similarly, some experiments imply that the memory capacities of men and women do not differ in any essential way, while the majority point to marked differences. Experiments with schoolchildren, in particular, tend to show that girls forget less than boys—that is, they make fewer omissions—but that they commit more unintentional falsifications and are therefore less accurate in detail.

Another point, more directly related to our purpose, deserves attention. A well-known psychologist showed three richly detailed pictures, carefully chosen to interest children, to a large group of boys and girls. Each picture was viewed for fifteen seconds, after which the children wrote a complete report of everything they could remember. They were then asked to underline those parts of their report of which they felt so absolutely certain that they would be willing to swear to them in court. The children exerted their best efforts, yet the results revealed that the underlined portions contained almost as many errors as the rest of the report. This experiment has been repeated many times, and although the effect is less pronounced in adults, it still appears in a surprising degree. Even the trained students of my own laboratory repeatedly commit this kind of unintentional perjury.

More refined experiments, conducted over a long period in my laboratory, have shown that the subjective feeling of certainty does not merely vary in degree, but differs fundamentally in structure and meaning from one individual to another. We found, above all, two distinct types. In one group, certainty in recollection depends largely on the vividness of the mental image. In the other, certainty rests on the harmony of the recalled image with other accepted memories—that is, on the absence of conflict when the experience is placed within a broader framework of past events.

Perhaps the most surprising outcome of these studies was the discovery that the feeling of certainty bears no fixed relation to the degree of attention originally given to the object. Even when we concentrate our attention with great effort on particular aspects of a complex experience, we may later feel more certain about elements we scarcely noticed than about those to which we devoted our full attention.

The more carefully we study the relationship between attention, memory, and certainty, the more complex it becomes. Both the common-sense psychology of the average juror and the limited psychological notions found in standard legal treatises on evidence collapse when confronted with a careful analysis of mental facts.

The sources of error, moreover, begin even before recollection takes place. Observation itself may be faulty or illusory; misleading associations may distort it; judgments may misinterpret experience; and suggestive influences may falsify sensory data.

The vast individual differences in powers of observation and judgment are well known. It is equally well known that some individuals, under favorable conditions, readily see what they expect to see. Conjurers, fakirs, and spiritualists rely on this fact, just as reading would be far more difficult if we did not habitually perceive the letters we anticipate.

Here, however, we may set aside distortions arising at the stage of perception, since these have already been discussed. Our present concern is solely with errors of recollection itself. From this narrower focus, we may now attempt to illuminate the problem from yet another perspective.

Many of us recall moments in which we pass through an experience accompanied by a distinct and almost uncanny feeling that we have lived through it once before. The words we hear, the actions we observe, appear familiar in every detail, as though they had occurred long ago. This experience is relatively rare among men, but extremely frequent among women, and there are few women who are entirely unfamiliar with it. An idea presents itself, closely bound to a strong feeling of recognition and remembrance, and yet this feeling rests on nothing more than an associated sensation—often the result of fatigue or emotional excitement—and has no objective foundation in the past.

For the psychologist, such experiences present no serious difficulty of explanation. But they should serve as a powerful warning to anyone who believes that a feeling of certainty in recollection guarantees objective truth. No new principle is involved when the ideas that enter consciousness arise from imagination rather than from external impressions. Any imagined thought may slip into awareness and carry with it that same peculiar sense of repetition, the illusion that it is merely the revival of an earlier experience.

A striking illustration of this phenomenon is familiar to anyone who has ventured into the somber literature of modern mysticism. There one finds countless reports claiming that prophetic fortune-tellers or inspired dreams have anticipated the future of an individual's life with astonishing precision and uncanny detail. Yet when these stories are examined critically, their marvel lies almost entirely in cases where the dreams or prophecies were written down only after the events had occurred. Whenever visions were recorded beforehand, the proportion of correct realizations remains well within the narrow limits of chance and ordinary probability.

In other words, there can be no doubt that reports of prophecies communicated after their supposed fulfillment are falsified—not deliberately, but through memory illusion. This does not in the least call into question the subjective honesty of the believer. The satisfied client of a skillful fortune-teller would readily swear to the accuracy of his recollection. Yet illusion it remains. He often feels equally certain that he told the dream to his family the next morning exactly as it occurred. Only when the family members themselves are questioned under careful examination does it become clear that the essential features of the dream diverged in every direction from the later event. The present reality reshapes the memory of the past prophecy, and each new occurrence is apperceived with the illusory coloring of having been foreseen.

We must constantly remember that a content of consciousness, taken by itself, bears no mark indicating whether it belongs to the past or is entirely new.

The feeling that an idea belongs to our earlier life may attach itself just as readily to a product of imagination as to a genuine reproduction of a former experience. And, of course, the opposite may occur as well: an actual past experience may return to consciousness stripped of any sense of familiarity, appearing like a newly invented thought.

This explains experiences that at first seem mysterious. The crystal-gazer, in a half-hypnotic state, believes he witnesses a free and inspired play of imagination. In reality, he experiences nothing more than a stirring of deeper layers of memory. Images rise into consciousness without any reference to their past origin and appear as timeless truths. Their apparent accuracy is surprising only because they are drawn from sharpened memory rather than from supernatural insight. Indeed, we constantly fill the gaps of our perceptions with fragments of reproduced memory and mistake these reproductions for immediate impressions. In short, from the content alone we can never be sure whether we are remembering, perceiving, or imagining. In these borderland regions, confusion is inevitable—and in the courtroom such confusion may have serious consequences.

There is yet another phenomenon familiar to everyone except, thus far, the courts. Memory exists in different types. In a crude and superficial classification, these may be described as visual, auditory, and motor types. Some individuals can reproduce a landscape or painting with vivid colors and sharp outlines across the entire scene, yet are unable to hear internally a melody or the sound of a voice. Others easily recall tunes and voices, hearing them inwardly with great clarity, and can scarcely read a letter without hearing the writer's voice in every word, while they are incapable of forming a clear visual image. Still others possess weak sensory imagery of both kinds and instead revive past experience primarily through tendencies of movement—of speaking, writing, or acting.

In reality, the number of memory types is far greater. Dozens of variations can be distinguished. Ask a group of friends to describe how yesterday's dinner table and conversation appear in their minds, and no two accounts will follow the same pattern. Just as we would not ask a near-sighted person to describe fine visual details of a distant scene, it is equally unsafe to ask a person with a predominantly auditory memory for precise visual recollections.

Yet no witness today is examined to determine in which directions his memory is likely to be reliable. He may be questioned about what he saw, what he heard, what he said, and how he acted—although even a simple test might reveal that his memory mechanism is well suited to one of these areas and utterly unreliable in the others, no matter how solemnly he swears to tell the truth.

The courts will have to learn, sooner or later, that individual differences among human beings can today be examined and measured by the methods of experimental psychology far more precisely than common sense or ordinary social experience would ever suggest. Modern law readily welcomes the discoveries of anatomy and physiology when it comes to identifying criminals.

Even the minute patterns of lines on a thumb are carefully recorded in wax. Yet no comparable effort is made to investigate the equally striking mental differences revealed by psychological experiments on memory and attention, feeling and imagination, perception and discrimination, judgment and suggestion, emotion and will—differences that have been clearly demonstrated during the past decade.

Other sciences have been far quicker to learn. It has been discovered, for example, that the psychological impulse underlying speech has, for each individual, a distinctive character of intonation and melody. Philologists immediately recognized the value of this insight and put it to brilliant use. They examined entire epic texts in which certain lines were suspected of being later interpolations.

Wherever the speech rhythm and intonation harmonized with the rest of the poem, the lines were accepted as genuine; where they did not, the lines were identified as later additions. Lawyers, however, could learn far more from psychologists about individual mental differences than philologists have already learned. They need only understand that the working of the mental mechanism within a personality depends on the constant cooperation of simple, elementary functions that modern laboratory methods can isolate and test.

Once these simplest elements are understood, the complex whole becomes a matter of necessity—just as the entire curve of a graph follows inevitably once its analytical formula is known for the smallest segment.

Psychological assistance, however, should not be limited to identifying different memory types and other individual traits. Experimental psychology has revealed a wealth of new facts about memory variation arising from attention and inhibition. We can now test, with remarkable precision, the fluctuating waves of attention through which ideas are strengthened or weakened.

Above all, we understand the inhibitory effects of excitement and emotion, which may completely alter the products of an otherwise reliable memory.

A concrete example may clarify the method by which experimental psychology approaches such problems. When doubt arises, the judge must decide on which side the evidence of fact carries greater weight. If it is assumed that both parties intend to speak truthfully, the judge may consider that one witness had more frequent opportunities to observe the facts, another may have observed them more recently; one may have seen them under especially impressive circumstances, another with fuller knowledge of the situation as a whole. Of course, the judge consults volumes of legal precedent, but these precedents merely record that earlier judges, relying on common sense, believed recency more important than frequency, or frequency more decisive than vividness, or perhaps the opposite.

This procedure resembles the way common sense dictates what kind of food is most nourishing. Yet no responsible physician would ignore the careful experiments of physiological laboratories that determine, with quantitative precision, the nutritive value of milk, eggs, meat, or bread. Judges overlook the fact that their own common-sense judgments could be transformed into precise measurements, the results of which might differ greatly from casual opinion. The task of the psychologist, of course, is to reduce complex facts to simple principles and elements.

An investigation devoted to the relative effectiveness of recency, frequency, and vividness was carried out in my psychological laboratory.

We used simple materials: pairs of colored papers and printed figures, colors combined with words, words with figures, colors with forms, and similar combinations. A series of ten such pairs was presented successively in a lighted field, each exposure showing one color and one two-digit number. One pair—perhaps the third—was repeated later as the seventh, giving it the advantage of frequency. Another—perhaps the fifth—was made especially vivid by presenting three digits instead of two.

The final pair enjoyed the advantage of recency, since nothing followed it to inhibit its retention.

After a pause, the colors were shown again, and each participant was asked to write down the figures he believed he had seen together with each color. Was the vivid pair remembered best? Or the frequently repeated pair? Or the most recent one? These experiments were conducted under many different conditions, with varying pauses, materials, series lengths, distributions, and participants. After years of work, clear and stable results emerged.

The relative value of these conditions for accurate recollection became measurable facts.

They may be refined and corrected by future research, but they are already far superior to the chance judgments of the lawyer who relies solely on intuition.

All of this lies entirely within the realm of normal, healthy mental life. Nothing here belongs to the province of the physician.

Where pathological amnesia destroys memory, or where hallucinations or fixed ideas rob testimony of its value, the alienist must speak, and the psychologist is no longer needed. It is precisely within normal mental life and its border regions that the progress of psychology can no longer be ignored.

No railroad or shipping company would assign a position of responsibility to an employee whose eyesight had not been tested for color blindness. Perhaps only one person in thirty or forty is unable to distinguish a red signal from a green one at a distance. Yet if such a person entered service without testing, his slight defect—harmless in daily life and possibly unnoticed unless he were picking red strawberries among green leaves—could be enough to cause a disastrous train wreck or a catastrophic collision at sea.

In the administration of justice, trains are wrecked and ships collide far too often because the law refuses to test the mental color blindness of a witness's memory.

And yet we have not even touched upon the factor that, more than any other, devastates memory and wreaks havoc upon even the most honest intentions of recollection: the power of suggestion.

Chapter of the End

Chapter–3.
The Scientific Path to Crime Detection

The chapter contrasts the brutal history of forced confessions with a modern scientific method based on psychological association tests, showing how hidden knowledge and inner conflict can be detected by measuring reaction times and subtle emotional changes when a person responds to certain words. Through case studies of criminals and ordinary individuals, it demonstrates that involuntary signs—such as delays, altered responses, breathing shifts, and small bodily movements—often reveal more truth than torture.

As old as the history of crime itself is the history of cruelty committed, in the name of justice, for the purpose of uncovering criminal facts. Human beings possess the ability to conceal knowledge and memory through silence and deception, and for countless centuries the infliction of physical and mental suffering has appeared to be the fastest way to loosen the tongue and force confession. Across thousands of years and in every region of the world, accomplices have been named, crimes admitted, and secrets revealed under threats and tortures that shattered the will to resist.

The imagination of the East devised more grotesque forms of torment than that of the West; the medieval Inquisition carried the system to a grim refinement; and even today the prisons of certain countries are said to witness practices that would be unthinkable elsewhere. And although outward forms have changed, can there be any serious doubt that even in the United States brutality still survives as a favored means of breaking down the mental resistance of the accused?

The thumb-screw may be gone, but lesser officials still possess innumerable methods for making a prisoner's existence miserable and intolerable, methods capable of exhausting endurance and crushing resolve. A rat secretly placed in a woman's cell may destroy her nervous balance and inner strength until she can no longer maintain her story. Blinding lights, cold-water hoses, sudden blows delivered out of sight—such practices are still reported to occur, even if many newspaper accounts of the so-called "third degree" are exaggerated. Worst of all are the savage shocks inflicted upon the terrified imagination of the suspect, blows directed not at the body alone, but at the mind.

Public conscience in modern society stands firmly opposed to such barbarism. This opposition does not arise merely from sentimental pity or aesthetic repugnance. Stronger than either is the deeply rooted conviction that such methods are ineffective in discovering the truth. Throughout history, innocent people have been driven under torture to accuse themselves and others; crimes that never occurred have been confessed; monstrous falsehoods have been invented simply to satisfy tormentors. Under pain and terror, a person may say anything that promises relief, and more dangerously still, the mind may lose its capacity to distinguish between genuine memory and illusion.

Enlightened juries have begun to recognize how profoundly justice is undermined by such practices. Not long ago, according to press reports, an American jury acquitted a suspect who had confessed in detail to the murder of a young woman after initially denying the charge. Detectives had taken the poorly dressed man to the undertaker's room, led him to the coffin, suddenly pulled back the covering to expose the bruised white face, and demanded abruptly, "When did you see her?" He collapsed to his knees, covering his face with his hands. They dragged him up, ordered him to place his hand on the dead woman's forehead, and continued firing questions at him, forcing him to touch her hair and cheeks. In a state of terror and mental collapse, he confirmed every suggestion put before him and even added invented details to his false confession.

The moral sense of a modern society rejects every such brutal method of seeking truth. Yet it remains painfully aware that the accepted means of uncovering facts are often inadequate. As social life grows more complex, it becomes easier to erase traces of crime and to conceal wrongdoing behind deception. Under these circumstances, it is astonishing—and difficult to justify—that lawyers and laymen alike have paid so little attention to the methods developed by experimental psychology in recent years, particularly the measurement of mental associations.

This neglect is not limited to association experiments alone. The same holds true for many other laboratory methods: the scientific study of memory and attention, feeling and will, perception and judgment, suggestion and emotion. In every one of these domains, psychological experimentation could render invaluable service to courts of law. Yet the study of associations is of particular importance in precisely those areas where the brutal practices of the third degree were once employed.

The chronoscope of the modern psychologist has become, and will increasingly become, for the investigator of crime what the microscope is for the physician. It reveals what is otherwise invisible, uncovering minute facts that allow a reliable diagnosis. Just as a physician examines sputum under magnification to detect tubercle bacilli, the legal psychologist may one day employ a mental microscope to determine whether deception or concealed knowledge exists within the suspect's mind.

The study of associations has attracted thinkers since the time of Aristotle, but only in the last century has it been pursued systematically, with an effort to uncover the laws governing mental connections. Everyone knows from everyday experience that memories link impressions together: a face recalls a name, a name recalls a face; one word evokes another; a smell or taste awakens a flood of recollections. From such familiar observations arose an entire systematic science. The associationist school attempted to explain the whole of mental life as the interaction of such associative processes.

There are associations of time and place, in which one experience recalls another that occurred alongside it. There are inner associations, where one idea evokes another through similarity, contrast, part-to-whole relations, or other internal links. The word "dog," for example, may summon the image of a particular animal, its name, the house where it was seen, the broader category "animal," the narrower "terrier," the coordinate "cat," a part such as "tail," a foreign-language equivalent, or even a painting in which dogs appear. The possibilities are endless. But psychologists were not content merely to classify these connections. Their central aim was to determine the conditions under which specific associations arise and to understand how factors such as frequency, recency, vividness, and the combination of experiences influence the resulting mental link.

Thus, in recent decades, experimental psychology has emerged as a true natural science, complete with its own laboratories in which mental facts are subjected to controlled investigation, just as physical facts are tested in physics or chemistry. Once experimental methods were applied, the study of associations entered an entirely new phase. In the laboratory, we are no longer dependent on the accidental material of daily life; we can design and regulate conditions precisely.

For example, a list of one hundred nouns may be read aloud to a subject, one after another, with the instruction to respond to each with the first word that comes to mind.

The resulting hundred associations are free from deliberate choice and reveal the natural paths of least resistance within the person's mind. These responses can then be analyzed statistically. A predominance of external associations suggests one type of mental organization; a dominance of internal associations suggests another. Frequent superordinate responses indicate a different intellectual structure than a prevalence of subordinate ones.

The experimenter may also study the influence of prior experiences. A story may be read or pictures shown before the association test begins, and the effect of this recent impression will immediately reveal itself in the associations produced. In this way, the possibilities for variation and insight are virtually unlimited, offering courts a humane and scientifically grounded alternative to the crude methods of coercion that once dominated the search for truth.

One aspect, however, rises above all others in importance: the ability to measure time in the connection of ideas.

Imagine that both my subject and I place small electrical instruments between our lips. The slightest movement involved in speaking either completes or interrupts an electric current that runs through a precision clock. The pointer of this clock moves around a dial ten times every second. One complete revolution therefore represents one-tenth of a second, and since the dial is divided into one hundred equal parts, each division marks one-thousandth of a second.

At first, the pointer stands still. The moment I move my lips to utter a word—for example, "dog"—the electric current is activated and the pointer begins to move. My subject, as soon as he hears the word, is instructed to speak aloud, as quickly as possible, the first idea that occurs to his mind. He may shout "cat." At that instant, the movement of his lips interrupts the current, the pointer stops, and I am able to read from the dial, in thousandths of a second, the exact time that has elapsed between my utterance of the word and his response.

Naturally, this measured interval includes more than the mere process of association. It also contains the time required to hear the word, to understand it, to form the impulse to speak, and to initiate the muscular movement of speech. Yet all these smaller components can be determined separately. For example, I can measure how long it takes when the subject does not form an association at all, but simply repeats the word I give him. If the simple repetition of the word "dog" requires 325 thousandths of a second, while responding with the associated word "cat" requires 975 thousandths, I may conclude that the difference—650 thousandths of a second—represents the time needed for the mental process of associating "dog" with "cat."

Through methods such as these, an exact and remarkably delicate study of mental associations has developed over the past twenty years.

By carefully observing differences measured in fractions of a second, psychologists have gained deep insight into the workings of the mind. The slightest changes in our mental connections can be detected and traced through these minute variations of time—variations that would remain completely unnoticed without precise measurement.

In recent years, the field has taken a decisive step forward: theoretical research has been placed at the service of practical life. Like many other branches of experimental psychology, the study of association has been adapted to real-world problems in education, medicine, art, commerce, and law. It is this last domain that concerns us most here—an approach that first emerged in Germany and has since been further developed both there and abroad.

Let us consider, for example, the case of a person suspected of having taken part in a crime. He declares himself innocent. He insists that he was not present when the offense occurred and claims no familiarity with the location. An innocent individual will not object to undergoing a series of one hundred association tests designed to demonstrate his innocence. A guilty person, however, cannot refuse either, for refusal would immediately suggest fear of self-betrayal.

He must submit, all the while confidently believing that no simple association experiment can force hidden facts from his mind. He remains on guard, convinced that his inner secrets are safe.

As long as the task requires nothing more than speaking the first word that comes to mind in response to another word, there is indeed no legal or practical reason to decline—especially while maintaining a profession of innocence. The experiment becomes immediately significant in three distinct ways once we introduce, among the hundred stimulus words, perhaps thirty that are more or less closely connected with the crime. These may refer to details of the location, to persons present, to possible motives, or to the alleged alibi.

The first focus of interest lies in the choice of associations themselves. Most people believe that they would easily prevent any dangerous word from escaping their lips. Yet the conditions of the experiment quickly shatter this sense of security. When a threatening association rises into consciousness, it strives instinctively to express itself. Admittedly, it may require skill and experience to detect its psychological influence, especially if the suspect possesses sufficient self-control to suppress the dangerous idea before it is spoken. But the suppressed idea does not vanish. It remains active in consciousness and subtly contaminates the next association—or perhaps the one after that—without the individual's awareness.

Suppose, for instance, that a man has murdered a woman in her room, yet insists that he has never entered her house. Beside her body stood a cage containing a canary bird. I therefore include the word "bird" among my test words. His mind, burdened with the gruesome memory of his crime, immediately calls up the association "canary."

Realizing the danger of such a response, he suppresses it and substitutes the harmless word "sparrow." However, a little later—perhaps at the next word, or the second or third—when I say "color," his prompt response is "yellow."

The image of the canary is still active in his mind, quietly exerting its betraying influence.

For this reason, the preparation of the word list demands psychological judgment and insight, especially when dealing with a subject capable of rapid self-control. In most cases, however, it is not even necessary to rely on later associations, for the primary responses to the critical words often reveal themselves clearly enough to provide significant evidence.

Yet the interest does not end with the first series of associations. A second line of inquiry opens when the entire list is repeated a second and even a third time. Suppose that after half an hour I again present the same hundred words, and the subject once more provides his responses. Analysis typically shows that most of the associations remain unchanged. The mere act of repeating the test strengthens the tendency to connect the same ideas as before. If the first response was "house" followed by "window," it will likely be "house" and "window" again.

However, a number of associations do change, and careful analysis reveals that these are usually the suspicious ones.

Words that are emotionally charged because of their connection to the crime stir up deep and complex clusters of ideas, producing new and shifting associations each time. In contrast, indifferent words form superficial connections that remain stable. To some extent, this variation in the dangerous associations is intensified by the suspect's own deliberate efforts. He feels uneasy about his initial responses and hopes that different words may better conceal his true thoughts—unaware that it is precisely this change that ultimately betrays him.

Yet the most decisive element lies in a third direction of inquiry—one that surpasses both the choice of associations and their consistency. This is the involuntary slowing of associations under emotional influence. A word that awakens emotionally charged memories will often require two or even three times as long to produce an association as an ordinary, neutral idea.

It should be stated at once that, for practical and especially for legal purposes, it is not usually necessary to measure these intervals in thousandths of a second. The time differences that reveal a troubled conscience or a concealed knowledge of facts are generally so pronounced that they can be measured easily in hundredths, or even tenths, of a second. Only the theoretical interests of psychology demand the refinement of dividing the second into a thousand parts. In the following discussion, therefore, all references will be made to differences measured merely in tenths of a second.

The absolute speed of association naturally varies from person to person. To connect familiar ideas such as "chair" with "table," or "black" with "white," may take more than a full second for a slow and deliberate thinker, while a quick and alert mind may complete the same task in half a second or less. For this reason, we begin by determining each individual's average association time.

All further interest then centers on deviations from this personal norm. An association time of one and a half seconds would be highly suspicious in a person whose usual speed is three-quarters of a second, while the same delay would be entirely normal for someone who habitually thinks more slowly.

Here again, it is important to note that the retardation does not always appear at the dangerous word itself. Often it emerges in a more revealing manner in the association that follows, or even in the one after that—an association that appears, on the surface, completely harmless. The emotional shock has disturbed the mental mechanism; the path of association is momentarily obstructed. The careful analysis of these secondary delays is the aspect of the method that demands the highest degree of psychological skill. A few illustrations drawn from real life may help to clarify the procedure.

An educated young man of eighteen lived in the house of his uncle. The older man consulted a nerve specialist concerning a mild nervous condition observed in the youth. During this consultation, he confided a troubling suspicion: the young man might be stealing. Money had repeatedly disappeared from a drawer and from a trunk. Until recently, suspicion had fallen only upon the servants. The police had been notified, and detectives had kept them under observation. Yet no proof had emerged. The uncle was deeply anxious to determine whether his new suspicion was justified, for if it were, he wished—out of consideration for the family—to keep the matter out of court.

The physician arranged for the young man to come for a neurological examination and proposed, as part of this medical inquiry, a series of one hundred association tests.

The doctor said "head," and the patient responded "nose"; "green" was followed by "blue," "water" by "air," "long" by "short," "five" by "six," "wool" by "cloth," and so on. The average time for these ordinary, emotionally indifferent associations was 1.6 seconds.

Scattered among the hundred words, however, were thirty-seven critical terms—words connected with the objects in the room from which the money had vanished, with theft and punishment, or with possible motives. When the word "thief" appeared, the association "burglar" followed, a response that seemed quite natural.

Yet it required 4.6 seconds to emerge. Similarly, "police" followed by "theft" took 3.6 seconds, and "jail" followed by "penitentiary" required 4.2 seconds.

In other cases, the dangerous word itself was answered with normal speed, but the emotional disturbance revealed itself in the delay that followed. For example, "key" was associated with "false key" in the usual 1.6 seconds.

Yet the next, entirely trivial pair—"stupid" followed by "clever"—suddenly expanded to 3.0 seconds. "Crime" brought "theft" promptly in 1.8 seconds, but the inner shock was so intense that the following harmless word, "cook," failed to produce any association at all for twenty full seconds. In a similar manner, "bread" was linked with "water" in 1.6 seconds; yet this choice, suggestive of prison fare, once again blocked the associative mechanism for the next trivial stimulus.

To pursue the analysis of this case in further detail would lead us too far afield.

It may be added, however, that when the same series of words was repeated later, the characteristic variations reappeared precisely in the region of the suspicious terms. Where "crime" had first produced "theft," it was replaced in the second trial by "murder." The word "discover" yielded "wrong" the first time and "grasp" the second. In contrast, the harmless words showed almost no change at all.

Finally, a subtle and comprehensive analysis of both the word choices and the time delays revealed enough detail to permit a clear diagnosis. The physician told the young man plainly that he had stolen.

The boy protested vehemently. The physician then pointed out the hidden indications disclosed by the associations—how the money had been used to buy a watch, how gifts had been purchased for his sister. Confronted with these facts, the young man confessed everything. The early discovery spared him imprisonment. Neither the brutal methods of coercive interrogation nor the rigid technicalities of legal evidence would likely have produced so complete and humane a result.

This case, of course, involved a highly sensitive individual burdened by the intense emotions of a guilty conscience. A hardened professional criminal would not display such strong emotional reactions and therefore might not exhibit such pronounced delays—at least not if he were unsuspecting and unaware of the true purpose of the experiment.

But what, then, would be the situation of a trained criminal, one without conscience, who knew in advance that the experiment was designed to determine whether he was lying or speaking the truth?

In such a situation, an entirely different group of facts must be taken into account. From a subject of this type, we should expect little or no lengthening of association time due to emotional disturbance. Instead, we would anticipate a marked delay caused by conscious effort—an intentional attempt to avoid suspicious or dangerous associations—provided the individual is anxious to conceal a damaging truth. The moment a critical word is spoken, such a person becomes alert. He does not allow the first idea that crosses the threshold of consciousness to pass freely to his lips. Rather, he pauses to examine it, to ensure that it is harmless, and, if it appears dangerous, to replace it with a safer substitute.

Experiment clearly shows that this process of vigilance and conscious approval consumes time.

The suppression of an unsuitable word and its replacement by a more acceptable one results in an even greater loss of time. No one is capable of constantly monitoring the innocence of his associations and yet producing them with the same rapidity as ordinary, unguarded ideas.

Where dangerous words show association times of unusual brevity, we are forced to assume that the subject makes no effort to suppress the truth. Such short times indicate that he allows ideas to arise and express themselves freely, without filtering, sanctioning, or conscious revision. Even the most skillful deceiver is thus betrayed by time differences that he himself neither notices nor can control.

As an illustration of this type, I may describe a series of experiments that I conducted over several days in a Western penitentiary with a self-confessed multiple murderer.

He served as the principal witness in a trial against a man whom his confession accused as an accomplice. Whether viewed from the perspective of the prosecution or that of the defense, the case presented a psychological problem of exceptional interest. This interest did not diminish when the jury's verdict ultimately established that the defendant was innocent and entirely unconnected with the witness's crimes.

At no point did either side question that the witness himself was one of the most persistent murderers of modern times. Nor could anyone deny that, throughout the trial, he appeared as an imperturbable witness—courteous in manner, calmly self-possessed, and marked by a quiet serenity that suggested a man who had found peace in God.

The first question confronting the psychologist was whether this confession was a deliberate chain of conscious falsehoods or whether the witness genuinely believed the story he told the court. No external evidence was capable of resolving this issue of his inner attitude.

It therefore seemed especially worthwhile to examine whether the association method might shed light on the matter.

I had the opportunity to observe the murderer directly while he was on the witness stand.

As my seat was at the small table reserved for the attorneys of the prosecution, he stood only a few feet away from me, within easy range of careful observation. I cannot deny that my initial impression, formed on that first morning, was distinctly unfavorable.

His profile—particularly the jaw—appeared coarse and brutal. I also noticed immediately the deformation of the ear, the irregular movements of the eyes, and the abnormal formation of the lower lip. That this was the profile of a murderer seemed to me not improbable; that this man could be a sincere religious convert, however, appeared highly doubtful. Yet I deliberately set aside these personal impressions. I relied instead on experiment. The testing began the following day.

This is not the place to present a formal scientific report of the nearly one hundred groups of tests and experiments that were conducted; such material belongs in scholarly archives. Most of the investigations concerned memory, attention, emotion, volition, judgment, and suggestibility.

Our interest here is confined solely to the association experiments and a few closely related tests. Accordingly, what follows represents only a small portion of the overall inquiry and deliberately excludes everything that does not bear upon the question of subjective truthfulness.

I told the witness quite frankly that my purpose was to examine his mind and discover what truly lay at the core of his inner life. He immediately declared himself entirely willing to submit to any test.

If he believed that, as an experienced poker player, he could easily conceal his inner thoughts and deceive me with practiced phrases and calculated falsehoods, I quickly reversed that assumption. I began with a few simple psychological demonstrations, well known to every student of psychology but entirely unfamiliar—and somewhat uncanny—to him.

For example, I covered one of his eyes and asked him to fix the other on a small cross placed on the table, while at the same time observing a coin that I moved to the side of the cross. Suddenly I told him that he would no longer see the coin. Indeed, it had disappeared.

Since he was unaware that everyone possesses a blind spot at the point where the optic nerve enters the retina, he was deeply impressed by what seemed to him my foreknowledge of a hidden defect in his vision.

On another occasion, I showed him a drawing that he perceived as a staircase. By observing his eye movements, I then told him that he no longer saw a staircase but an overhanging wall—and again he was astonished at my apparent ability to know what was occurring in his mind. I employed similar tactile illusions, and before long he was completely under the impression that I possessed unusual scientific powers.

Only then did I begin the actual experiment. I informed him that I would call out fifty words, and that each time he heard a word he was to reply as quickly as possible with the first idea that occurred to him. I asked him not to choose his responses deliberately, but to let them come without reflection. I added that everything of importance would reveal itself through the ideas he produced. My first word was "river," and he responded "water." Then came "ox," to which he answered "yoke"; "mountain," answered by "hill"; "tobacco," answered by "pipe." To him, it appeared that the entire interest of the experiment lay in the choice of words, and he saw that I carefully wrote down his responses.

In reality, I was doing something more. I was measuring, in fractions of a second, the interval between my utterance of each word and his response.

Between "river" and "water," eight-tenths of a second elapsed; between "ox" and "yoke," six-tenths; between "tobacco" and "pipe," again eight-tenths. In general, seven to eight-tenths of a second proved to be the remarkably brief standard time for these associations involving familiar ideas.

Interspersed among the fifty words, however, were many that bore a direct relation to his criminal history and to his professed religious conversion—words such as confession, revolver, religion, heaven, jury, death, Bible, pardon, railroad, blood, jail, prayer, as well as the names of his victims and of his alleged accomplices. It must be remembered that he was firmly convinced that I possessed a special power to uncover, through his spoken words, the true tendencies of his mind. Had he wished to conceal anything, he would necessarily have been on constant guard to prevent any treacherous word from slipping out. If a word like "confession" were suddenly introduced among harmless ones, he would not have allowed the first association to escape unchecked. He would have suppressed it—perhaps fearing that something like "confession" followed by "falsehood" might betray him—and substituted a safer response. However quickly such suppression might occur, it would inevitably consume additional time, at least one or two seconds more. He would have taken this time freely, since he had no reason to suspect that time itself was being measured or that it played any role in the experiment.

The results, however, revealed a striking and significant fact. The dangerous words, taken as a whole, showed no delay whatsoever in the associative process.

After "tobacco"—"pipe," the word "confession" followed with "truth," and again in eight-tenths of a second—a duration far too brief to allow for deliberation, approval, correction, or conscious choice.

It is a span of time that permits only the immediate expression of the first idea that arises. "Heaven"—"God" appeared in less than a second, as did "religion"—"truth," "blood"—"knife," "governor"—"executive," "witness"—"stand," "minister"—"pulpit," and "mine owner"—"mine." Only more abstract words such as "pardon"—"peace" or "death"—"end" required about one and a half seconds, a duration still insufficient for genuine inhibition or second thought. Even the names of his accomplices and of his victims elicited associations in less than nine-tenths of a second.

The fact that these associations emerged with minimal delay—at a speed that made conscious suppression impossible—while the witness firmly believed that his words would expose his true inner nature, constitutes powerful evidence.

It indicates that this man was making no conscious effort to hide anything and that he himself genuinely believed in the truth of his confession.

Had these experiments been conducted before his confession, the results would have been entirely different. He would have faltered at nearly every third word, and many of his associations would have required three seconds or more.

Despite his best efforts, he would have been unable to overcome the fear of self-betrayal, and this fear would have slowed his associations in a manner that would have exposed him unmistakably. Yet it was not only the brevity of the association times that was revealing; the very choice of the associations made it clear that, in an almost unbelievable way, a mild and indifferent serenity had taken possession of his mind. His criminal past no longer seemed to concern him in the least.

For example, I presented him with the name of a city in which, according to his own confession, he had last poisoned a victim and destroyed the victim's house with dynamite. In his mind, however, the place no longer connected itself with murder. In less than a second, it was associated simply with "ocean." The association times made it evident that no genuine emotion accompanied any of his memories of crime. He neither possessed nor simulated a guilty conscience. The emotional delay that ordinarily marks suspicious associations in the average criminal was, as anticipated, completely absent in this habitual murderer.

This absence of emotional retardation does not imply a lack of feeling altogether. On the contrary, my experiments demonstrated the opposite. His sensitivity to physical pain was, like that of most criminals, well below average. A deep pinprick produced no reaction, and his general sense of touch was dull, while his vision and hearing were remarkably acute. Yet despite this insensitivity to bodily pain—he had never been seriously ill—he displayed a marked sensitivity to the immediate perception of suffering in others. Simulation can be excluded here, as I measured involuntary reactions. He genuinely shuddered at the thought of inflicting pain on another person.

I have no reason to doubt that he possessed this psychological sensitivity throughout his life, and this does not contradict the fact that he inflicted suffering on many. Nearly all his crimes were committed in an impersonal manner. He did not confront his victims directly. He constructed infernal machines, placed dynamite in mines, and set bombs beneath gates, thinking of the suffering of the victims no more than a toy manufacturer might think of the happiness of the children who play with his products. He assured me that during fifteen years of atrocious acts, he never once struck another person with his fist; such an act, he said, would have offended his nerves.

In many respects, he displayed a surprisingly gentle emotional disposition. He showed refined aesthetic preferences, selecting delicate color combinations as his favorites among many presented to him. Dark blue appeared to be his preferred color, while anything showy or loud in dress was distasteful to him. He even claimed that he rarely consumed strong alcoholic drinks, explaining that a single glass of beer made him drowsy.

And yet, despite all this, his emotional life was essentially dead. The consistently minimal association times would otherwise be impossible. It may also be added that even if his religious conversion was sincere, his so-called religion lacked any deep or vital feeling. It was entirely utilitarian in character; he served God because he believed that God would reward him after death.

In this case, the association experiments fully achieved their purpose. They provided a clear answer to a clearly defined question—one that could scarcely have been resolved by other forms of evidence. The experiments demonstrated that the murderer was not attempting to conceal anything. This, of course, was only the first issue to be settled. From the standpoint of subjective truthfulness, which concerns the psychologist, to the proof of objective truth, which concerns the court, there remains a long and difficult path. It was entirely possible, for example, that his condition resulted from pseudo-religious autosuggestion, from systematic illusion induced by detectives and lawyers, from hypnosis, or from mental disease. All these possibilities required careful experimental examination, and they constituted the major portion of my investigation. They do not belong here, however, since they bear no direct relation to the method of association measurement, which is the sole focus of this discussion.

The theoretical value of this method is, of course, independent of the practical importance of the particular cases in which it is applied. Multiple murderers are rare, but even the simplest act of wrongdoing can demonstrate the effectiveness of the method just as convincingly. No contrast could be sharper than that between the brutal criminal with his dynamite bombs and a delicate young girl whom I had examined shortly before.

She was anemic and neurasthenic and found herself unable to concentrate on her studies for her college examinations. She came to me seeking psychological advice. I questioned her closely about her habits of life, and among other things she assured me that she ate wholesome and sufficient meals and was not permitted to buy sweets.

I then began a series of psychological experiments, and among them, almost casually at first, I introduced some trivial association tests. Her average association time was slow, nearly two seconds.

Very soon, the word "money" elicited the response "candy," and it appeared quickly, in 1.4 seconds. In itself, this was unremarkable. But the next word, "apron," harmless by any standard, required six seconds to produce an association, and the response was "apron"—"chocolate." Both the excessive delay and the inappropriate association indicated that the previous stimulus had produced an emotional disturbance. The choice of the word "chocolate" made it clear that this disturbance stemmed from the intrusion of the word "candy."

"Apron" itself had no emotional significance; it merely followed in the wake of the candy-related excitement.

I took this as a guiding clue. After introducing twenty indifferent words, which gradually restored her emotional equilibrium, I returned to the topic of sweets. By this time, she was evidently on her guard. When I again introduced the word "candy," she required 4.5 seconds to respond, and the result was the naïve association "never." This was the first response that was neither a noun nor an adjective.

Up to that point, her associations had treated the words as simple objects. "Candy," however, was perceived by her as an accusation or reproach, something to be denied. She was entirely unaware that this shift from a descriptive to a defensive mental attitude was itself highly suspicious. On the contrary, she seemed satisfied with her answer, for the subsequent associations were brief and appropriate.

After some time, I approached the subject again indirectly. The seemingly innocent word "box" quickly brought the equally innocent "white." Yet I immediately recognized it as a candy box, for the next word, "pound," produced the association "two," and the following word, "book," after a long delay, yielded the inappropriate response "sweet."

Once again, she was unaware that she had revealed the course of her imagination.

Over the course of three hundred associations, I repeatedly varied the subject, and throughout the entire process she remained unconscious of the fact that she had provided me with all the information I needed.

When I finally told her that she skipped lunch every day, ate almost no regular meals, and instead consumed several pounds of candy daily, her astonishment exceeded even her embarrassment. With tears, she eventually made a full confession. She had concealed her unwise diet because she had promised her parents not to spend money on chocolate.

This accurate diagnosis enabled me to offer the appropriate suggestions, and within a few weeks her health and strength were fully restored.

This seemingly trivial case, with its harmless and foolish offense, illustrates how psychological detective work can be valuable far beyond the boundaries of the courtroom. It is often a matter of serious concern for both educators and physicians to uncover concealed thoughts, and the so-called "third degree" of the classroom or the consultation room could, in many instances, be replaced by association experiments.

On such a foundation, the nerve specialist would frequently be able to arrive at an accurate and helpful diagnosis without relying on any explicit "confession," and without arousing even the slightest suspicion in the patient that the true source of the difficulty had been uncovered.

Experience has convinced me that this method can reveal facts of which even the patient himself is unaware.

Ideas that are deeply rooted in the inner life, yet cannot be voluntarily recalled by a simple effort of memory, are sometimes brought to expression through the mechanical procedures of association testing.

It appears that once a series of associations has been produced under the pressure of responding as quickly as possible, the mind enters a state of reduced inhibition. In this condition, suppressed and forgotten ideas are suddenly freed and rush into consciousness.

This phenomenon becomes increasingly significant as we learn—under the guidance of the Vienna School—that one of the most troublesome nervous disorders, namely hysteria, arises primarily from suppressed emotional ideas and can be cured by reawakening these restrained thoughts. Hysteria is, in essence, "strangulated emotion," and it disappears when the forgotten emotional experiences are once more brought into conscious awareness.

One hysterical woman, for example, invariably became mute after sunset. Another was unable to take any food except liquids. A third was constantly tormented by hallucinations of the odor of tobacco. Every physician is familiar with dozens of such symptoms. None of these patients understood the cause or origin of her affliction. Gradually, however, the physician uncovered the suppressed ideas that had been denied expression and had produced their destructive effects in an inhibited form.

The woman who lost her voice at night had once, many years earlier, sat at sunset beside her sick father's bed and had forcibly suppressed every sound so as not to disturb him. The moment this long-forgotten scene was brought back into consciousness, her voice returned.

The woman who could not eat solid food had been compelled, years before, to suppress her disgust while dining at the same table with a man afflicted by a repulsive disease. When this initial experience was consciously revived, she was again able to eat normally.

The woman haunted by the smell of tobacco had once, in a smoke-filled room, learned by chance that the man she loved was devoted to another woman.

She had been forced to suppress her emotional reaction because others were present. When the odor was once more consciously connected with that first strangulated emotion, the hallucination vanished.

Hysterical contractions and anesthesias, pathological impulses and inhibitions, can all be relieved once the long-forgotten emotional ideas from which they originated are brought to light. It is precisely here that the association method may prove especially useful.

The psychologist who seeks to uncover the hidden connections of ideas may, through this technique, not only protect the innocent and expose the guilty, but also restore health and strength to the shattered nervous system.

Nevertheless, our principal interest lies in the legal significance of this method.

When applied with the skill that only prolonged laboratory training can provide, it becomes a magnifying glass for the most delicate mental processes, capable of unveiling the secrets of the criminal mind.

At present, of course, such methods have no formal standing in the courts, and there is probably little desire to increase the already large number of "experts" in criminal trials. Yet justice ultimately demands that truth be distinguished from falsehood.

The time will come when the methods of experimental psychology can no longer be excluded from the courtroom. It is worth recalling that the use of stenographers in trials once encountered vigorous resistance, whereas today the shorthand record of court proceedings is taken for granted.

The assistance of the psychologist will become no less indispensable.

The crude practices of the "third degree," in all their forms, belong to the Middle Ages, and much of the legal wrangling over technicalities in the admission of evidence appears to many observers equally outdated.

The methods of experimental psychology are working in the spirit of the modern age.

The "third degree" may brutalize the mind and force either genuine or fabricated secrets into the open.

The measurement of association times, by contrast, is cleaner, swifter, more scientific, more humane, and more reliable in revealing the truth that justice seeks.

Naturally, we are still only at the beginning of its development. The method remains imperfect in many respects, and when clumsily applied it may be misleading.

There is no rigid formula that can be mechanically fitted to every case. All this merely underscores a broader principle:

just as bodily facts must be examined by the chemist or the physiologist, so mental facts must also be examined—not by the layman, but by the scientifically trained psychologist, equipped with the discipline and experience of the psychological laboratory.

Chapter of the End

Chapter–4.
The Involuntary Language of Emotion

This chapter explores how emotions unconsciously reveal themselves through involuntary physical signs such as changes in movement, breathing, pulse, and other bodily reactions. It explains how experimental psychology scientifically measures these hidden emotional responses and examines their possible role—and limitations—in legal investigations.

When a young woman blushes at the mention of a certain name in the family sitting room, we feel certain—no matter how firmly she may deny it—that the person in question is not entirely indifferent to her heart. When she opens a letter and grows pale while reading it, she may insist that the matter is trivial; we know better. And if she converses with you in a manner that suggests her full attention belongs to you and to every word you speak, it may still be enough to notice that her fingers are nervously playing with her fan, that her breathing has become deeper and more agitated, and that her eyes have grown restless since a particular guest entered the room. You realize at once that she is scarcely listening to you at all and is merely waiting for him to approach.

If he does not come, she may be a master of simulation. The practiced smile may never leave her lips. Yet you will hear her disappointment in the tone of her voice, and you may even detect it in the widening of the pupil of her eye. Hidden feeling, yes, often betrays itself against the will of even the most accomplished actor in life.

It may be comparatively easy to suppress the conspicuous movements by which emotions usually express themselves. We need not rage in anger or collapse in grief; we may restrain laughter and tears, and cultural habits alone may dictate restraint—a New Englander will not express emotion as a Southern Italian might. Yet the lips, hands, arms, and legs, which lie largely under voluntary control, are never the sole witnesses to the drama unfolding within. If they remain silent, other signs will speak.

The poets have always known this truth. Throughout the dramatic literature of all ages, one recurring motif appears again and again: the involuntary expression of emotion. The horrifying memory of a terrible deed may seem sealed within a character's mind, yet when he is brought back to the scene of his crime, it reveals itself in his pallor and trembling, in the vacant stare of his eyes, and in the breaking of his voice. There is scarcely a tragedy by Shakespeare in which such unintentional signs of hidden excitement do not play a decisive role. Likewise, the comedies of all ages repeat the same motif in lighter form, exposing the secret entanglements of love and society. The helpless stammering of the excited lover betrays everything his carefully chosen words seek to conceal.

The signs that made Hamlet certain of his mother's guilt have not gone unnoticed by those who pursue criminals in real life. The suspect who turns pale in the presence of his victim while pretending not to recognize him, or who breaks into tears when hearing the account of crimes he vehemently denies, is already half condemned in the eyes of the prosecutor.

When the conspiracy against Dreyfus sought to fabricate evidence against him, much emphasis was placed on the fact that he trembled and could barely write while phrases from the alleged treasonous document were dictated to him. Much of what both police officers and suspects refer to as the "third degree" relies precisely on such bodily signs of a guilty conscience. To force the accused to collapse under the weight of his own emotions is regarded as the triumph of this misuse of legal authority.

It even appears that certain superstitions of barbaric times, which claimed to reveal guilt through miraculous signs, occasionally contained a kernel of truth. These practices often relied on seemingly mysterious indications that were, in fact, bodily effects of emotion. Primitive life sharpens the observation of such symptoms. One of the most daring gunmen of the American West once told me that when he was threatened by a mob, he deliberately behaved as though he were constantly spitting. He adopted this manner because it discouraged the crowd; they interpreted it as fearlessness. As he put it, a frightened man cannot spit—the emotion of fear dries the mouth and throat.

Yet it is obvious how uncertain and dangerous such crude methods must be. Justice cannot rest on a detective's claim that a suspect blushed, trembled, or breathed heavily. Such judgments would hardly be superior to the superstitious verdicts of earlier centuries. Too many people see what they expect to see, and very different emotions may produce strikingly similar bodily symptoms. If such superficial observations were allowed serious weight in determining guilt or innocence, the door would be open to arbitrariness and grave injustice.

This leads inevitably to a crucial question: can science come to our aid? Can it determine with accuracy and reliability what remains vague and uncertain in the casual impressions of police officers? More than that, can science make visible what is too subtle and fleeting to be perceived by ordinary observation? The bystander notices the outward signs of overwhelming emotion—but can science, and in particular experimental psychology, bring to light the traces of the entire play of feelings, from the faintest and most transient to the most violent emotional storms? Can it reveal not only the obvious upheavals of consciousness, but also its most concealed suggestions?

This question is all the more pressing because the idea of the psychological expert in the courtroom can no longer be dismissed. Mental life—perception and memory, attention and thought, feeling and will—plays far too central a role in judicial proceedings to justify excluding the counsel of those who devote their professional lives to the scientific study of these processes. Moreover, the progress of modern psychology in recent years has been too rapid and too substantial to be ignored with the condescension once appropriate when psychology was largely speculative and psychological laboratories did not exist.

Today, the psychologist works with the methods of exact science. The task demanded here is fully in harmony with those methods. The essential problem is whether fleeting emotional symptoms can be objectively recorded, and whether expressions too subtle for ordinary perception can be reliably captured. This, precisely, is what the laboratory psychologist continually strives to accomplish. Whether measuring the duration of mental processes, analyzing complex ideas, investigating the senses, or studying acts of will, the psychologist is always engaged in linking vague inner experiences with external, measurable facts that can be recorded—and in illuminating those aspects of mental life that ordinarily escape notice.

In the domain of feelings and emotions, experimental psychology has been no less successful than in any other area of inner life. If we limit ourselves to the particular problem that concerns us from a legal standpoint, we may say with confidence that the psychologist is indeed able to register the symptoms of inner excitement—and more than that, to demonstrate the effects of feelings and emotions that leave no trace detectable by ordinary observation. Even the most refined psychological instruments, however, ultimately refer to the same bodily processes that visibly reveal emotion in everyday life: we blush in shame, grow pale and tremble in fear, shiver in horror, weep in grief, perspire in anxiety, leap in joy, feel heat rise and fists clench in anger. In all these states, blood vessels contract or dilate, the heartbeat changes, glands alter their activity, and muscles function irregularly. The difference is that scientific instruments allow us to perceive changes that are almost microscopic.

We may illustrate several directions along which such investigation can proceed. Let us begin with one of the simplest processes: ordinary movements of the arm. Do feelings influence them? My answer comes from a personal record kept many years ago—a small diary, devoid of sentimentality, filled instead with figures. Its purpose was to preserve the results of about twenty brief experiments, each requiring roughly half an hour.

I always carried the necessary apparatus with me and repeated these experiments three or four times daily over several months. I experimented whenever daily life placed me in a characteristic mental condition—emotion, interest, fatigue, or any state that might be psychologically significant. One of these experiments was as follows. I attached a small instrument to the lower part of my waistcoat. With this device, I slid my right hand—thumb and forefinger together—along an edge, moving both outward and inward.

I had trained myself to reproduce, from memory, distances of four and eight inches. Under normal conditions, with my eyes closed, my hand traced these distances with precision. The apparatus automatically recorded whether the movement was too long or too short. Hundreds of such measurements were entered in my diary, each accompanied by a note describing my mental state at the time.

When I analyzed the results after six months, a clear relationship between feeling and movement emerged. The records revealed essentially three fundamental pairs of emotional states. There were pleasure and displeasure, excitement and depression, and gravity and hilarity. The figures showed that in states of excitement both outward and inward movements became too long, while in depression both became too short. In pleasurable states, outward movements were exaggerated and inward movements shortened; in displeasure, the reverse occurred. In conditions of gravity or hilarity, no consistent change in the length of movement appeared, but the rhythm and speed of the action were noticeably affected.

For the first time, three distinct groups of feelings were thus differentiated and recognized through three distinct patterns of bodily behavior. After I published these findings, others, approaching the problem from different perspectives, arrived at similar divisions of feeling. Some reduced the system to two basic groups, while others—an opinion I do not reject—maintained that pleasure and displeasure alone are fundamental, and that qualities such as excitation or calmness are secondary. Today, however, I am inclined to recognize a larger number of simple feelings, each with its own characteristic form of movement. These considerations become important when the psychologist attempts to explain emotion and asks to what extent sensations themselves contribute to feeling.

What matters here is the central fact that pleasurable and unpleasurable moods betray themselves through opposite movement impulses of which we remain entirely unaware. In hundreds of trials, I intended to execute precisely the same outward and inward movements, yet the experiments revealed the illusion. We all know that joy reinforces outward movement—the boy swings his cap and stretches his whole body—while anger produces opposite impulses, contraction being the typical expression. Experimental results show that such impulses operate even when we neither know nor display them. Bring a person before a recording apparatus, and it becomes possible to determine from his movements alone, without his awareness, whether his inner world is bathed in sunshine or clouded by gloom.

Unintentional movement can reveal emotion in yet another way. Whatever awakens feeling also initiates action toward the object of interest. All forms of muscle reading or thought reading rest on this principle. The ouija board of spiritualists is a familiar illustration. If we wish to record such imperceptible movements with precision, we may use an automatograph—a plate resting on metal balls that follows every impulse of a hand placed flat upon it. Through an attached mechanism, even the slightest motion is traced on a slowly moving surface. If the arm is suspended in a loop from the ceiling, the hand will respond even more freely to minimal impulses without the subject's awareness.

Ask a person to concentrate intently on a particular letter of the alphabet, then arrange twenty-five lettered cards in a semicircle before him. His hand, resting on the automatograph, will soon reveal a faint impulse toward the chosen letter, though he remains entirely unconscious of it. Similarly, if a witness or a suspect stands before a row of men and insists that he recognizes none of them, the automatograph may nevertheless point toward the individual he truly knows—the one whose presence stirs emotional excitement.

In some cases, even simpler recording methods suffice. If the hand rests on a rubber bulb or on a capsule covered with elastic membrane, the slightest finger movement will compress the air within. Through a tube, this pressure reaches a small chamber that moves a lever, and the lever records the motion. The accused may believe himself perfectly still, yet when he hears the dangerous name of a crime scene or an accomplice, his involuntary muscular contraction is faithfully recorded. With suitable technique, even the faintest trembling can be captured by attaching a small cap to a finger.

Emotional interest may also betray itself through movements that are not ordinarily under conscious control, such as those of the eyes. I discovered that our eyes may act independently of our awareness. Suppose a subject looks straight ahead while I present a card bearing an emotionally neutral word. We agree beforehand that after reading the card he will close his eyes, turn his head slightly to the side, and then open his eyes again. The experiment shows that, under these conditions, his eyes follow the direction of his head. Repeated trials confirm this result.

Now I substitute a word that I know, from earlier experience, carries emotional significance for him. The outcome changes abruptly. He reads the word, closes his eyes, turns his head, opens his eyes again—and without his knowledge, his eyes have not followed the head movement. They remain directed toward the emotionally charged word. The backward rotation of the eyeballs betrays the presence of feeling.

In this way, I may show a suspected individual one indifferent object after another, and his eyes will faithfully follow his head. But present an object connected with the crime, present at the scene, or belonging to the victim, and if he recognizes it, his eyes will cling to it during and after the head movement. Long experience has taught the police that not only do the eyes seek the scene of emotional disturbance, but the entire person seems magnetically drawn to the place where the crime was committed. Dostoevsky has portrayed this truth with profound insight, showing how the murderer, almost against his own will, returns to the scene of his deed and thus moves inexorably toward his fate.

We are still speaking, of course, of movement, yet we enter an entirely different domain when we turn to breathing. Inspiration and expiration can be recorded with the finest precision, and psychology now commands a variety of elegant methods for this purpose. Perhaps the simplest instrument is the pneumograph, which consists of a tube made of spiral wire and covered with rubber, fastened to the chest by ribbons. Each movement of breathing lengthens or shortens the tube, forcing a portion of the enclosed air into a small capsule. The flexible cover of this capsule responds to the changing air pressure and moves a recording lever—usually a long straw that magnifies the motion. The tip of this straw lightly touches the smoked surface of a slowly revolving drum, tracing a delicate wave line that reveals even the most subtle features of respiration.

It is an easy matter to measure every aspect of such a curve: its length, height, angle, regularity, and rhythm. Each variation corresponds to a change in the speed, strength, distribution, or pause of the breath. Once such refined methods are employed, the intimate connection between feeling and respiration becomes unmistakable. Pleasure, for example, tends to make breathing weaker and more rapid; displeasure makes it stronger and slower; excitement strengthens and accelerates it; acquiescence weakens and slows it. Yet such generalizations barely suggest the richness of the phenomena. Every ripple in the stream of mental life is mirrored in the breathing curve—whether it is an agreeable or disagreeable taste or odor, stirring or depressing news from outside, or a sudden fancy arising within.

The same is true of the heartbeat, which can be measured through the blood wave in the arteries by means of an instrument known as the sphygmograph. This device may be attached, for instance, to the wrist. A delicate lever presses lightly against the arterial wall at the point where a physician would feel the pulse. The lever is connected to a thin rubber membrane covering an air chamber, and changes in air pressure are transmitted to a long straw that traces an enlarged record of the pulse on a steadily rotating drum driven by clockwork. Each heartbeat has its own distinctive form, length, and height. When pulse and breathing are recorded simultaneously on the same drum, it becomes immediately evident that even a single ordinary inspiration alters the pulse: the heartbeat differs during inhalation and exhalation. Emotional states exert an even stronger influence. Once again, however, broad statements—such as pleasure strengthening and slowing the pulse, displeasure weakening and accelerating it, or excitement making it both stronger and quicker—remain crude abstractions that fail to capture the full complexity of the changes.

Another approach lies in observing the distribution of blood within the body. With the aid of the plethysmograph, for example, we can examine how much blood flows into a limb. The arm is placed in a large tube filled with water and sealed by a rubber cuff. Any increase in blood supply causes the arm to swell slightly, altering the pressure exerted on the water. This pressure change is transmitted through air to a recording lever, and each emotional excitation finds expression in the blood flow of the limb. Such instruments have been standard equipment in physiological laboratories for decades. It was therefore almost comical to read, not long ago, in numerous American newspapers that I had invented the sphygmograph, automatograph, and plethysmograph in a single summer; they might as well have credited me with inventing the telegraph the previous spring. What truly belongs to recent years is not the invention of these instruments, but their systematic application to the study of emotion.

We can go even further and point to expressions of emotion that lie entirely beyond the reach of ordinary human senses. If a weak galvanic current from a battery is passed through the body by placing the hands on copper plates, a sensitive galvanometer can detect the slightest variations in electrical resistance. Experiment shows that such variations occur whenever the brain is excited. Emotional disturbances influence resistance, apparently because the activity of the sweat glands in the skin—regulated by the nervous system—alters the electrical conditions. A single word that stirs emotion may make the galvanometer needle quiver at once. There is scarcely a more uncanny betrayal of our innermost mental life.

We may also consider the knee reflex. A small hammer drops from a constant height onto the tendon below the knee, producing a reflex jerk whose angle can be measured. Experiments demonstrate that this angle changes with emotional excitement. Evidently, impulses from the brain influence the spinal mechanisms responsible for the reflex, and emotion modifies their function. Even body temperature appears to be affected by emotional states. Physicians know well how a patient's feelings can alter the course of a fever, and experimental evidence suggests similar, though subtler, effects in the normal condition.

There is thus no real doubt that experimental psychology can supply everything the court might demand. It can objectively register the symptoms of emotion, freeing observation from the uncertainties of casual judgment. It can trace emotional reactions through involuntary movements, breathing, pulse, and other processes where ordinary perception fails entirely. And yet, despite all this, a certain caution—and even skepticism—regarding the practical application of these methods is still justified.

In the first place, research into the bodily registration of emotion remains in its early stages. Many difficulties have yet to be overcome, and contradictions persist among the findings of different investigators. Above all, we still know too little about individual differences to base legal decisions today on breathing or pulse curves alone. The phenomena are exceedingly complex, and much further work is required before practical situations can be reliably interpreted.

Secondly, experimental methods do not yet provide a secure means of distinguishing the emotional agitation of a guilty conscience from the anxiety of innocence. An innocent person—especially one of nervous temperament—may become just as emotionally disturbed on the witness stand as a criminal when the victim or the instruments of the crime are mentioned. Fear of unjust condemnation can influence muscles, glands, and blood vessels as strongly as genuine guilt. Experimental psychology must not aspire, with refined instruments, to reproduce the injustice of barbaric interrogation practices.

For the present, the most reliable application of experimental emotion methods appears to lie in determining whether a suspect has prior knowledge of a particular person, place, or object. If an unfamiliar name is introduced, for example, the method is dependable: the innocent individual, who has never heard it, will react no more strongly to that name than to any of several others; the criminal, who recognizes it as that of a witness or accomplice, will show unmistakable emotional signs. Even here, however, it would be unwise to draw rigid boundaries. The rapid progress of experimental criminal psychology may well resolve tomorrow the difficulties that still stand in the way today.

Chapter of the End

Chapter–5. False Confessions and the Tragedy of Misguided Justice

This chapter explores how confessions and eyewitness accounts can be dangerously unreliable. Through real cases and psychological research, it shows how suggestion, emotion, and mental strain can distort memory and even lead innocent people to believe in their own guilt, warning that justice must carefully question the certainty of human recollection.

What I am about to recount is a painful story—a strange and haunting tragedy of our own recent past. I am deeply convinced that it represents not only a tragedy of crime, but also one of human error and failed justice. My responsibility as a psychologist compels me to speak of it, for the tragedy of yesterday may easily return tomorrow, perhaps in another form, if its lesson remains unlearned. I am the last person to seek for the modern psychologist any special privilege to intrude into the ordinary affairs of practical life. Too often the so-called "new psychology" has been treated as a universal remedy, a kind of intellectual jack-of-all-trades. Psychology has been expected to supply cures for all the shortcomings of our schools; it has become a fashionable word in literature and religion, in social unrest and economic distress. The public can scarcely imagine the burden this places on a psychologist's correspondence—letters from the superstitious and the mentally unbalanced, reports of uncanny and mysterious happenings, and demands for explanations wherever experience appears strange or inexplicable. In such cases, the psychologist is expected to label the occurrence, classify it, and give his official endorsement that such marvels may indeed happen.

It is difficult to read such letters without wishing that the writers would consult a detective instead. No psychological explanation is appropriate until the facts themselves are firmly established by methods for which the scholar is not trained. A psychologist, accustomed to the pursuit of truth, is often least prepared to detect the countless sources of deception and delusion that a skilled attorney may uncover with ease. In this sense, the psychologist may often wish that the detective had been consulted instead of himself.

Yet this does not prevent him, at times, from regretting precisely the opposite—that society relies on the detective alone, when the psychologist ought also to be heard. As the scientific analysis of mental life advances through experimental, physiological, comparative, and clinical methods, we increasingly recognize how subtle and complex the inner connections of the mind truly are, and how inadequate popular psychology must be when it confronts unusual mental states.

In the case I have in mind, the accused was swiftly branded as "crazy" by the press, and the label was repeated with careless certainty. Day after day, my mail brought a chorus of indignant letters. Efforts by the defense to stay the execution through a petition to the Supreme Court failed. One week later, the young man was hanged. And yet, if scientific conviction may speak honestly in the name of truth, I must say again that he was executed for a crime of which he was no more guilty than you or I. The only change since then is that, as I have been reliably informed, many of the most sober-minded citizens of Chicago now share this sorrowful belief.

From the beginning, I felt certain that no individual was deliberately at fault. Court and jury had plainly done their utmost to determine the facts and weigh the evidence. They could not be expected to possess expert knowledge of rare and abnormal mental conditions. The proof of the alibi appeared sufficient to some, insufficient to others. Many facts admitted of differing interpretations. All hesitation, however, was swept aside by one seemingly unassailable argument: there was a complete confession.

Given the extraordinary tension of the public mind at the time, the sensational tone of the press was, perhaps, understandable. Chicago had been shaken by a series of brutal murders. Too often the criminal had escaped punishment. Now, at last, a man had confessed. He, at least, would not evade the gallows. For years no murder case had so profoundly agitated the city. As long as calls for further psychological investigation appeared to the public merely as "another attempt to cheat justice," or as a threat to weaken court procedure and discourage faithful officers of the law, newspapers could scarcely be expected to resist the tide of popular feeling.

I therefore accepted without resentment what was described as a noble outburst of civic indignation when a leading newspaper summarized the matter in these terms: *Illinois has quite enough of people with an itching mania for attending to other people's business without importing impertinence from Massachusetts. This crime itself, no matter who committed it, was one of the frightful fruits of a sickly tampering with the stern administration of the law. We do not want any guidance from irresponsible Harvard theorists to tamper still further.* This judgment, it seems to me, strikes very near the heart of the matter—except for the phrase "no matter who committed it." It does matter profoundly who the criminal was—whether it was the man who was hanged, or someone else who remains free even today.

If one examines the countless reports in search of a genuine argument for the young man's guilt, everything ultimately reduces to one assertion, endlessly repeated: that it would be "inconceivable" for an innocent person to confess to a crime he had not committed. Months have passed since his life was taken, since thousands crowded Michigan Street, blocking it from Clark Street to Dearborn Avenue, waiting for the undertaker's wagon to leave the jail yard. The discussion has long since shifted into the realm of theory. Perhaps now, with the heat of passion cooled, the moment has come to ask calmly whether it is truly inconceivable that an innocent person might confess to a crime of which he is entirely ignorant.

The question is not merely academic. Tomorrow it may again demand a practical answer, when another vulnerable mind may drift into a false confession and society, reassured and complacent, may once more rely upon it—hypnotized by the dangerous belief that "murder will out." The history of crime in Chicago alone proves that murder does not inevitably reveal itself. The task of the court is not merely to extract guilty thoughts, but to avoid planting them in an innocent mind.

In criminal procedure, no form of evidence seems more decisive than a confession—provided it is trustworthy and clearly established. When an accused person explicitly admits guilt, it appears that the goal of justice has been reached. And yet, in every age and every nation, experience has urged caution in the acceptance of confessions. The intensity of this caution has varied across periods. Perhaps this fluctuation reflects the nervous condition of society at different times. In earlier centuries, when science was unaware of hysteria and neurosis, social instinct may nevertheless have guarded against their dangers. The chief objection to confessions, however, has traditionally been social rather than psychological: the possibility of promises, threats, or pressure exerted by others.

Such influences have differed across times and social conditions. Occasionally, the motive of self-sacrifice—confessing in order to protect another—has also played a role.

In short, there is no shortage of social reasons that make it entirely conceivable for an accused person to confess falsely, even of his own accord. In minor offenses, in particular, promises and threats remain, even today, frequent sources of false self-accusation.

To these motives we may add another. Even a person in full possession of his mental faculties may confess falsely when confronted with a disastrous combination of circumstantial evidence. Faced with what appears to be overwhelming proof, he may hope that a confession will secure mercy.

Every lawyer recalls the celebrated Boorn case in Vermont, in which two brothers confessed in detail to the murder of their brother-in-law and described how they disposed of the body—only for the supposedly murdered man to return alive years later.

The evidence against the brothers seemed so crushing that they believed their only chance lay in reducing the charge from murder to manslaughter through a false confession.

To this category we may also assign many of the historic confessions from the Salem witchcraft trials. In those cases, the closest relatives urged the accused women to confess, seeing no other path to survival. These tragedies stand as enduring reminders that confession, however persuasive it may appear, is not synonymous with truth—and that justice, when blinded by certainty, may become its own most dangerous adversary.

Those dark chapters of New England history offer far more than a single explanation of false confession. They reveal, step by step, an entire spectrum of mental states, leading from deliberate calculation to complete alienation, passing through every borderland of confusion and disintegration of the mind. Even the advice given by the closest relatives of those accused as witches was often not based on confidence or affection. To them, the absurd accusations themselves appeared sufficient proof of guilt, and refusal to confess seemed mere obstinacy. They urged the imprisoned women to confess, convinced that unwillingness to do so showed that their minds had been wholly surrendered to Satan.

In many cases where the accused yielded, it was not from cowardly fear or mere self-preservation, but because their judgment had collapsed and their minds were in complete submission and exhaustion.

There can be little doubt that some of those who confessed truly believed themselves guilty. Contemporary reports further agree that, once these individuals resolved to confess, they fabricated their stories with remarkable ingenuity and coherence, carefully aligning them with the statements of their accusers and adding details that lent an air of credibility.

Ann Foster of Salem Village, for example, confessed in 1692 that the devil had appeared to her repeatedly in the form of a bird. She further declared that Goody Carrier had made her a witch. Carrier, she said, threatened that if she refused, the devil would tear her to pieces and carry her away. She claimed to have attended meetings of witches in Salem Village, traveling on sticks, and elaborated the narrative in full. Yet Ann Foster was not insane. The terror of the accusations had overwhelmed her distressed mind. Today we would say that a dissociation had set in: the emotional shock shattered her normal personality, and a secondary personality began to form, constructing a coherent life story from the grotesque superstitions suggested to her through relentless and hypnotic examinations.

Thus, false confessions motivated by hope or fear, by promises or threats, by calculated reasoning or passive surrender, gradually shade into others given with sincere conviction—confessions shaped by emotional upheaval or by overpowering external influence. Even sheer physical exhaustion often weakened the mental resistance of the accused witches. Prolonged interrogations continued for hours, forcing prisoners to stand or depriving them of sleep until their strength was broken. In such a state, they finally assented to accusations of having signed the devil's book.

At the opposite pole of society, far removed from these cruel court procedures, stand the hospitals for the mentally ill, guided by humane intentions. Yet even there, the sound of reckless self-accusation is familiar to anyone acquainted with the wards of melancholic patients. There is no judge and no jury—only physician and nurse—yet the torment endured by the melancholic patient may surpass any judicial punishment. He reproaches himself for sins he never committed, for crimes he had never imagined. A friend once died, and now the patient believes he poisoned him. A fire destroyed the town, and he is certain he set it. He has committed the unforgivable sin. Minor faults from his actual past assume monstrous proportions, and long-forgotten mistakes awaken with overwhelming anguish. He accuses himself of deceit, cruelty, and monstrous intentions, elaborating the details of his imaginary crimes with growing precision.

In the modern courtroom, when the physician utters the grave diagnosis of melancholia, such self-accusations lose all judicial relevance. The hospital doors close behind the patient. He may still testify regarding others, but his confessions of personal guilt can never be accepted as evidence. Because the symptoms of melancholia and related depressive states are readily recognizable, there is little risk that such pathological fabrications will be mistaken for genuine confessions of crime. Yet this raises a critical question: does this safeguard extend to illusory confessions arising from temporary abnormal states in minds that are not diseased?

Hysterical and autohypnotic conditions may coexist with otherwise normal behavior. Pseudo-confessions can emerge in individuals who are not mentally ill.

A slight dissociation may occur—insufficient to summon medical attention, yet powerful enough to profoundly influence admissions made by the accused. Does the court possess adequate means to convey to the jury that such subtle, non-pathological mental variations must be weighed with care?

Courts are careful to examine whether a crime was committed under conditions of mental responsibility. Yet the mental state of witnesses receives far less refined scrutiny.

Cross-examination focuses largely on the time of the crime, often overlooking the witness's mental condition during the trial itself.

Most neglected of all is the psychological state of the defendant during the proceedings. It is commonly judged by the crudest standards of everyday psychology, which assumes the mind to be normal so long as the individual is neither insane nor intoxicated.

Such assumptions are deeply misleading. No psychological mechanism remains unchanged when a witness testifies under oath or when a defendant faces a jury. These changes usually remain within the bounds of normal life—normal meaning compatible with the individual's life purposes—but they are real nonetheless. Only the psychologist is fully aware of their direction and influence. Practical life is satisfied with simple labels: the witness was excited, anxious, timid, self-important, or eager to persuade. How far perception, memory, imagination, emotion, will, attention, judgment, and self-awareness were altered by the situation is rarely examined and would be irrelevant in the majority of cases.

Yet there is no sharp line separating mental disease from normal variation. No mental trait belongs exclusively to pathology. Everything observed in asylums is composed of the same elements that constitute ordinary mental life. What differs is proportion and balance. A single trait may be exaggerated or suppressed to such an extent that harmony is destroyed. Mental illness is a caricature of normal personality. Just as a caricature exaggerates a nose or teeth that are otherwise ordinary, mental disorder magnifies ordinary feelings, impulses, memories, or imaginations until balance is lost.

Because mental disease introduces no fundamentally new elements but only distorts existing ones, there is nowhere a clear boundary between normal traits and pathological excess. The brooding immobility of the melancholic patient is unmistakable, yet the pessimistic temperament of many healthy individuals already contains the seeds of such despair. Self-reproach and guilt without guilt are common even among the mentally sound. From these mild temperamental tendencies to complete alienation stretches a continuous scale of depression, passing through neurasthenic and neurotic states.

Determining where temperament ends and irresponsibility begins is extraordinarily difficult because of this broad borderland. Public opinion, along with court and jury, tends to claim this entire region for normal life and to recognize disturbance only when unmistakable disease appears. Modern psychology, however, increasingly insists that careful analysis of this borderland is essential if justice is to be served. In other domains, courts readily acknowledge scientific progress. It is instructive to observe how neurasthenic conditions are now recognized in civil law as genuine bodily disturbances, whereas not long ago they were dismissed as imaginary complaints. Psychology, too, has reached a stage where its advances must be acknowledged.

Every mental function shows a similar continuum. We know the superficial, distractible individual whose attention constantly wanders, yet mania represents only an extreme exaggeration of this trait. We recognize the impulsive sanguine temperament, the sluggish will inhibited by inner resistance, the stubborn mind impervious to argument, and the suggestible mind that believes every printed word. Each of these traits can grow into its pathological caricature, and between originality of character and mental collapse lie countless intermediate steps.

A psychological trait becomes dangerous when imbalance renders the individual incapable of pursuing life's purposes. Doubt about the reality of the external world may be found both in the asylum and on the philosopher's platform.

Whether the doubter is a patient or a philosopher is revealed not by the doubt itself, but by its consequences. The philosopher integrates doubt into a coherent life plan; the patient's life is shattered by it.

It is precisely within this vast and delicate borderland that false confessions are born—and it is here that justice must learn to tread with the greatest care.

The close correspondence between slight, normal variations of mental life and the gravest disturbances is perhaps nowhere more clearly revealed than in the field of memory. We differ from one another not merely in the strength or weakness of retention, nor only in the domains in which memory excels—one remembering names, another faces, one figures, another sounds—but also in the irregularity of memory's disturbances and illusions. Just as no two human faces are exactly alike, so no two memories are identical in structure or function. Even unusual varieties of memory may remain entirely within the bounds of mental health.

I may illustrate this with a personal example. I possess absolutely no memory for the mental processes of sleep; in other words, I have never experienced a dream. When I speak of dreams in my university lectures on psychology, I do so much as a blind person might speak of color. And yet, mental processes clearly continue in my sleeping brain as in others. Friends have often observed that when I am awakened abruptly and questioned, I first give absurd replies filled with fragments of the preceding day. But once fully awake, not the faintest trace of these thoughts remains in my memory.

This rare type of memory is not pathological, for it does not interfere with the purposes of my life. Indeed, one might argue that those who dream are rather to be pitied, for dreams may blur the boundary between imagination and the real past.

If most people were dreamless, the dreamers themselves would likely consult nerve specialists, and their condition would be placed in the borderland between normality and hallucination. Dreams are, after all, hallucinations rendered harmless only because the impulses to act are inhibited during sleep.

No mental function shows such breadth of variation within normal limits as memory—neither in its positive aspects of retention nor in its negative aspects of forgetting. Forgetting, in itself, is neither a defect nor a symptom of disease. On the contrary, life would be impossible without it. We would be overwhelmed if we retained every face glimpsed in the street or every advertisement read in the paper. The mind must constantly sift its contents. Indeed, we expect normal memory to follow the lead of imagination. We do not insist on recalling experiences exactly as they occurred.

Perception itself contains gaps that imagination fills with fitting associations. When we remember a landscape, we want a complete picture; we care little whether the wave had precisely that curve or the tree exactly that number of branches. Memory functions well when it selects, discards what is irrelevant, and supplements the rest with imaginative additions that recreate the experience as meaningful.

Yet it is evident that this process of suppression and supplementation becomes dangerous when it grows excessive. If we fail to recall past experiences and, at the same time, are deceived by illusions of false memory, we lose our footing in social life. At that point, only institutional care can protect us from ruin. But where does the boundary lie? When do forgetting and imaginative completion pass beyond safety? Nowhere is the borderland broader, and nowhere is it more crucial for the psychology of the courtroom.

For a long time we may still remain within normal limits. Simple fatigue may weaken resistance and allow deceptive illusions to creep into memory. Emotional excitement may have a similar effect. The solemnity and importance of standing before a court can, in many minds, produce a state especially favorable to suggestion, allowing confused ideas to cluster around emotionally charged thoughts. Even an impressive or leading question may distort memory. More powerful still is the suggestiveness of the entire situation, particularly its social elements. Suggestion permeates education, art, politics, and religion. It is normal, and yet it suppresses objective memory to a high degree. Gradually, these influences lead into the borderland. Fatigue becomes exhaustion; mild excitement deepens into the affective influence of alcohol or drugs; the ordinary suggestiveness of authority gives way to hypnotic intrusion or autohypnosis.

None of this is necessarily pathological, yet the distortions of memory may already be so extensive that the value of reported recollections is profoundly altered.

The unreliability of memory under such conditions has nothing to do with the honesty or intentions of the witness. Most people know very little about the workings of their own minds. Many are unaware of their peculiarities. Some do not even know they are color-blind, or that they lack forms of imagination common to others. A colleague once asked me to hypnotize him after discovering, at the age of forty, that he possessed no visual memory; he hoped hypnosis might supply it, though he had never missed it before reading of it in a psychological text. Only recently, a young woman consulted me who had reached college age without realizing that others do not hear voices when alone. She had experienced them since childhood and assumed this was universal. The average person is unfamiliar with the subtleties and deceptions of memory. These variations rarely concern the physician, but psychological examination today offers something like mental X-rays, illuminating inner processes that ordinarily remain unseen.

We must remember that our knowledge of ourselves is itself a function of memory. Psychologically, we know who we are through the remembered continuity of our actions and experiences. This self-consciousness is subject to the same vulnerabilities as memory in other domains. Our own actions, sensed through muscle and movement, are no more securely remembered than scenes we have seen or words we have heard. When memory of one's past disappears entirely, pathology is evident. When self-related memories split and form secondary personalities, the physician's domain is unquestioned. Yet even here, the most severe disintegration is reached by gradual steps from everyday experience.

Each of us is a different personality in different situations. The man at work is not the man at home; the traveler on vacation is not the same person he is at his desk; the speaker at a political meeting is not identical with the spectator in a theater. Each context brings new impulses, new clusters of memory, new emotional groupings that reshape the whole mental landscape. Normally, the core of personality remains intact, and we move easily between these states.

This harmony allows effective action. But under certain conditions, a new personality may gradually emerge, defined by its own impulses and memories, increasingly detached from the former self. Emotional shock or captivating impressions may revive forgotten memories or elevate imaginative constructions, around which dissociated elements of the mind organize themselves into a new personal system.

At first, this altered self may hardly be distinguishable, yet its emotions and memories may be subtly distorted. Over time, the change may deepen until the individual himself cannot explain the shifts in his attitudes, judgments, or self-awareness. This borderland between normal personality variation and pathological disintegration demands the most serious attention in the courtroom.

With this in mind, I return to the distressing Chicago case. Dr. Christison has presented the entire matter in a compelling pamphlet that few can read without concluding that an innocent man died by the rope because of false confessions. For present purposes, it suffices to recall the essential facts. On January 12, 1906, a young married woman was brutally assaulted and murdered in Chicago. Her body was discovered by the unfortunate defendant, lying face downward on a manure pile in a barnyard. The barn stood about half a block from his home, and he had gone there in the ordinary course of caring for his father's horse. Upon seeing the body, he immediately reported the discovery to his father, who notified the police.

When officers arrived, they found the woman's hat near her feet but no signs of a struggle. Her purse, shopping bag, and muff were missing. Around her neck was a tightly drawn copper wire, twisted at the ends. The young man appeared not to have slept, and suspicion quickly fell upon him. Testimony described him as thoughtful, obliging, and unusually good-natured, yet often showing marked dullness. He avoided the company of women, was widely regarded as trusting, credulous, and absent-minded, and alternated between cheerful and gloomy moods. His most notable defect, according to acquaintances, was a lack of initiative. He worked regularly with his father as a carpenter. When he was taken to the police station, he was immediately told that he was the guilty man. He denied the charge entirely.

The police now began to press him relentlessly, suggesting his guilt with increasing insistence. Then, quite suddenly, he began to confess. Once started, he was willing to repeat his confession again and again, each time enriching it with additional details. "At about 6:30 I took her in the alley. I wrestled with her and lost my senses. She wanted to run," and so the story continued, expanding with every repetition. On this foundation alone, he was condemned to death.

Such was the state of affairs when my opinion was requested, as previously described. I could not avoid the conviction that all the external indications contradicted the jury's interpretation. The alibi presented by the young man's friends appeared to me convincing. Everything suggested that the woman had been murdered elsewhere by an unknown assailant and that her body had been dragged during the night, by the copper wire twisted around her neck, from another street into the barnyard. The so-called confessions themselves struck me as absurd, contradictory, and precisely what one would expect from the involuntary elaboration of a suggestion planted in the mind. His entire life history, together with the expression of his face, strongly supported the suspicion that his mind had entered a dissociated state at the moment the confessions began. To me, it appeared a typical case from that wide borderland region in which a neurotic mind constructs an illusory memory of its own past actions.

After the most careful scrutiny that the available written and printed material allowed, I wrote, in June, in my much-abused letter, that the confessions must be untrue and that the condemned man had no connection whatsoever with the crime. I added at once: "It is an interesting case of dissociation and autosuggestion; careful treatment would probably be required to reintegrate his dissociated mind and thereby awaken a clear memory of his real experiences."

Yet even as I expressed this firm conviction, I was troubled by an uneasy sense that something remained unexplained. I could not understand how the abrupt transition from denial to confession had been brought about. Certainly there had been sharp and insistent questioning by the police officers, but from my experience I could not believe that such interrogation alone, without some sudden external shock or overpowering fascination, could produce so rapid a collapse and disintegration of personality.

Only a short time earlier, a woman had come to me who exhibited strikingly similar memory gaps spanning several days, which she had filled with imaginative fabrications. She too could not comprehend how her personality had changed so abruptly. When I hypnotized her, the explanation became clear. She had been in a nervous and severely over-fatigued condition when her physician bent over her, and the sharp sunlight reflected from his eyeglasses struck her eyes. At that instant she experienced it as a shock; the glasses seemed suddenly enlarged and uncanny. From that moment onward her consciousness split, and the remaining fragment of her personality developed a pseudo-memory of its own.

I also recalled a case of religious conversion recently analyzed and described by Dr. Prince. A young woman, previously sunk in extreme distress and restlessness, suddenly passed into a state of joyful excitement and ecstatic happiness. She interpreted this transformation as a spiritual conversion to health. The change in her mental personality was indeed astonishing. She herself could not recall anything that might have caused it. Yet when the physician hypnotized her for therapeutic purposes, the entire sequence became clear. She had entered an empty church in a state of hopeless despair. As she stood there, her despondency deepened. Her gaze then fixed upon one of the shining brass lamps, and suddenly everything changed. She fell into a trance-like state in which scattered memories of her early life and of happier times rushed into consciousness, each accompanied by strong emotion. These long-forgotten feelings of happiness persisted and reshaped her entire mental state.

Had there been, in the Chicago case, any such captivating visual stimulus—a reflection like that from an eyeglass, or a shining object like the brass lamp—everything would have been intelligible to me. Without such a factor, I could not fully account for the suddenness of the defendant's mental collapse. When I wrote my letter, I felt certain that, had I been able to hypnotize the condemned man, I would have discovered that some unexpected stimulus had intervened and abruptly severed the normal mental connections. I expressed this wish repeatedly at the time. I could not foresee that the explanation I sought would be provided only a few days later by events themselves.

The unfortunate youth suddenly awoke from the dreadful spell. The period of disintegration vanished from his memory, and his normal mental connections reasserted themselves. The same newspaper that had insisted he must be guilty because no innocent man would ever confess to so brutal a crime published, a few days later, a long report beginning as follows:

"With death on the gallows only six days away, he now asserts his innocence of the atrocious murder. He declares that he has absolutely no memory of having made a confession to the police. He states that his only recollection of the coroner's inquest is of seeing a revolver pointed at him. 'I saw the flash of steel in front of me,' he said. 'Then two men stepped before me. I can remember no more than that. Someone afterward told me who the man was, but I had not seen him at all, and I do not recall seeing any others until after I had seen the revolver. I suppose I must have made those statements, since everyone says I did, but I have no knowledge of having made them, and I am innocent of the crime. From the time of my arrest, I do not believe I was myself for a moment until after I was brought here to the jail. Everything from that time is a blur, a blank. I can see through the blur the time at the station, when the police would bring me in repeatedly and tell me that I had done it. I know the very first thing the inspector said to me was, "You did this." I knew I had not done it, yet I do not know what I said or did during that time. I wondered why a revolver was pointed at me.'" It would be absurd to suppose that this sudden clarification was a fabricated tale designed to escape punishment. Throughout the weeks of his half-dazed condition, he had never made the slightest effort to weaken his confessions or to defend himself. Moreover, this dull and simple young man would have been utterly incapable of inventing, on his own, a narrative that so precisely matched the clinical experiences familiar to physicians of nervous disorders and the psychological observations of dissociation. "I saw the flash of steel in front of me." From that instant onward, everything became blurred and blank. This was the missing link in the chain of evidence proving his innocence.

He could not possibly have understood that the flash of steel functioned psychologically like the shining brass lamp in Dr. Prince's case or the reflected eyeglasses in the other instance. He reported the facts naively, truthfully, and with every mark of authenticity. He would have been incapable of fabricating such scientifically exact observations. What he could fabricate, under suggestion and confusion, was fully revealed in his earlier "confessions"—a contradictory mixture of improbabilities and psychological impossibilities.

Six days later, the sentence of death was carried out.

Chapter of the End

Chapter–6
The Subtle Power of Suggestion in the Courtroom

In this chapter, the author explores how suggestion subtly shapes human thought, memory, and perception—especially within the courtroom. Through striking experiments in hypnosis and psychology, he reveals how easily beliefs can be implanted, memories distorted, and judgments influenced without conscious awareness. What appears to be sincere testimony or rational decision-making may, in reality, be guided by unseen psychological forces.

I was visiting a large city for the first time when I had the opportunity to observe a series of hypnotic experiments conducted by a colleague, a physician specializing in nervous disorders. He invited me to witness the treatment of a woman who had been deeply hypnotized for a local nervous complaint. In all other respects, her mental life appeared entirely normal. She was a woman of wealth, education, and social standing.

While she was in hypnotic sleep, the physician suggested to her that she should return later that afternoon. Upon finding us both present, and as soon as he took his watch from his pocket, she was to declare her intention of making a last will in which I should become the sole heir to her entire property. She had never seen me before, and I had been introduced under a fictitious and wholly indifferent name. When she awoke and left the office, she showed no sign of recognizing me or taking any interest in my presence.

At the appointed hour she returned, apparently without knowing herself why she had come. In the drawing room she found, besides her physician and myself, three or four additional observers who wished to follow the course of the experiment. She showed no embarrassment. She explained casually that she had happened to pass the house, felt so much improved that she wished to report her condition to her doctor, and wanted to ask whether there was any objection to her attending the theatre that evening. I began an ordinary conversation with her about the opera. For ten minutes or more we spoke of music and drama as naturally as if we had met at a social gathering. There was nothing in her words, manner, or expression that seemed in the least unusual.

Then my friend asked the time and, as arranged, drew his watch from his pocket. For a brief instant she hesitated. She began to speak with a slight stammer, then suddenly continued fluently. She said that she had not expected to meet so many people, but that her true purpose in coming was to inform me that she had chosen me as her heir and that she now wished to proceed with the making of her last will.

Up to this point, her conduct was simply the mechanical execution of the post-hypnotic suggestion. What followed, however, was far more instructive. I told her that there must be some mistake, as she could not possibly know me. I mentioned a fictitious city and claimed that I lived there. Without hesitation, she replied that she had spent the previous winter in that very city, had met me there daily in the streets, and from the beginning had resolved to leave me all her property. I objected that she had never spoken to me. She immediately answered that she had encountered me repeatedly in society in that same city.

I then pointed out the apparent absurdity of leaving her fortune to a stranger rather than to her children. She responded at once that she had reflected on this for years, that wealth would be a burden rather than a blessing to her children, and that she was convinced I would use the money for philanthropic purposes. One by one, the others present offered arguments against this extraordinary decision. For each objection she produced a carefully reasoned and persuasive reply, as though the matter had long been settled in her mind.

Finally, I told her plainly that she had been hypnotized that morning and that the idea of making this will had been implanted in her mind by the physician's suggestion, in full view of the witnesses. She smiled calmly and replied that she knew this perfectly well, but that she accepted the suggestion only because it happened to coincide entirely with plans she had cherished for more than a year. She added that she would have written to me soon even if I had not come to the city. She declared herself unwilling to tolerate further doubt regarding her sincerity and offered to swear under oath that her resolve predated the hypnosis.

To bring the scene to a close, she demanded paper and pen and wrote a codicil leaving her entire estate to the fictitious man from the fictitious town. The physicians present signed as witnesses. I placed the document in my pocket, turned the conversation back to the theatre, and after a few minutes it was evident that she had entirely forgotten the episode. She once again treated me as a complete stranger. When I asked whether she knew the city I had mentioned, she replied that she had merely passed through it once by train. When she left the house, she had not the slightest recollection of the document in my pocket, which we afterward destroyed together.

Had I been present that afternoon as an uninformed observer, I should have been completely deceived. I would not have thought of questioning her testimony or seeking further confirmation. Everything appeared coherent and consistent with the single idea implanted in her mind. Her memories were reshaped, her emotions reversed, her tastes transformed, and her entire life history reorganized and supplemented by unrestrained imagination—yet all this occurred with perfect sincerity and conviction. With the exception of that single externally imposed decision, the entire construction was the product of her own mind.

If a suggestion entered consciousness as an isolated foreign element, detection would be easy. Its contradictions with established memories and habits would betray it at once. But this is precisely the sinister power of suggestion: it immediately spreads to neighboring ideas and emotions and brings the entire mental life of the person under its influence.

Life rarely offers such striking demonstrations, and the risk that judges or jurors might be misled by such extreme phenomena seems small. Only a few individuals can be hypnotized to the point where a post-hypnotic suggestion becomes so dominant. Yet it cannot be emphasized too strongly that such extreme disturbances differ only in degree from the most ordinary mental processes.

The grotesque effects of deep hypnosis merely exaggerate the subtle workings of suggestion that pervade everyday life, descending by imperceptible steps to the mild and familiar influences that shape our thinking—those casual exhortations we encounter daily, urging us to adopt opinions, habits, or preferences without reflection.

The psychologist does not require hypnosis to demonstrate how suggestion alters memory. In one experiment, a picture of a farmer's room was shown individually to about forty children and adults. Each observer examined it carefully and was then asked to report what he remembered in response to detailed questions. The picture contained many easily recognizable details. Neutral questions produced accurate answers: how many persons were present, whether the room had windows, what the man was doing. There were indeed people and windows, and the man was eating his soup.

Other questions, however, referred to objects not present in the picture and varied in their degree of suggestiveness. Asking whether there was a stove in the room was less suggestive than asking directly whether the observer had seen the stove. There was no stove. Questions followed about houses visible through the windows or a lamp hanging from the ceiling. The results were striking. Only fifty-nine percent of the answers to these suggestive questions were correct. Time and again, observers confidently reported objects that had never existed, inventing details in immediate response to the form of the question, despite having just observed the picture and having no personal interest in falsifying the account.

Here, in its simplest and most harmless form, we see the same mechanism at work that, under graver circumstances, may mislead witnesses, distort memory, and influence the course of justice itself.

The experiments further demonstrate that resistance to suggestion is markedly weaker in young people than in adults, and weaker in girls than in boys. Yet it must be emphasized that all these experimental subjects were tested under conditions of complete emotional calm. Such conditions are rarely present on the witness stand, where the solemnity and tension of court proceedings create a state of excitement that may reduce the resistance of even mature adults to the level ordinarily seen in children. Above all, the experiments reveal that suggestion exerts its influence not vaguely or generally, but in the most minute and concrete detail.

Once a subject has agreed, for example, that there is a stove in the room, he is immediately prepared to answer further questions with equal confidence: where is the stove standing? One places it on the left, another on the right; one imagines it in the corner, another against the middle of the wall. Each follows, without awareness, the path of least resistance offered by his own imagination.

The experiments permitted a precise gradation of the suggestive power of different forms of questioning. The farmer's wife in the picture wore a red gown. It was often sufficient merely to ask whether the gown was blue or green to erase the red entirely from memory. With increasing suggestiveness of the questions, the readiness to elaborate invented details increased steadily.

Experiments of this type have been conducted in many countries, with individuals of different ages and professions, using widely varied material. The results have been strikingly uniform. Again and again, the capacity of a suggestive question to undermine accurate memory proves alarming. Anyone who has studied the protocols of psychological laboratories must feel that many courtroom cross-examinations differ only in setting from these controlled tests. There is often nothing more suggestive to certain witnesses than a skillfully framed question.

Its influence may begin long before opposing counsel has time to object to an overtly leading inquiry.

The distorting effect of suggestion, moreover, need not wait for memory to come into play. Perception itself can be altered by suggestion. Experimental psychology demonstrates this fact in countless variations. Such laboratory experiments may appear trivial and remote from the complexities of real life, offering nothing more than schematic demonstrations. This impression is mistaken. Their strength lies precisely in their simplicity. All experimental sciences progress by reducing complexity to its essential elements.

The physicist does not wait for a thunderstorm to study electricity; the small electrical apparatus on his laboratory table teaches him far more clearly which factors determine an electric discharge. Artificial schematization isolates causal relations. In the same way, the psychologist does not require the chaotic interplay of emotions and prejudices found in real life to understand suggestion. The essential mechanisms reveal themselves just as clearly in slight distortions of perception produced by simple experimental material.

For instance, if I place thirty small gray squares of paper on one side of a table and the same number on the other, and ask a subject to decide, without counting, which side contains more squares, I can easily arrange matters so that he sees more on whichever side I choose.

His judgment may depend on grouping: the same number of pieces suggests different quantities depending on whether they are arranged in orderly rows or scattered irregularly; divided into small clusters or combined into a single mass; enclosed by a frame, accented by a few ink marks, or set against a bright background. In short, numerous secondary factors suggest erroneous judgments regarding quantity.

Yet these harmless experiments expose precisely the same influences by which political parties before elections create misleading impressions of their relative strength. A small patch of bright color on my laboratory table can exert on my subjects the same moral effect that torchlight processions and brass bands exert on suggestible voters.

An even more striking demonstration is offered by another experiment. We prepare a series of cardboard boxes of varying sizes, from a few inches to several feet, and adjust them so that all weigh exactly the same—the smallest filled with iron, the largest with straw. Each box has an identical handle.

When lifted one by one with closed eyes, they feel equal in weight. But when the subject lifts them with open eyes, the impression of weight is immediately governed by the visual suggestion of size. The smaller box now seems several times heavier than the larger, and no conscious effort can eliminate the illusion. The distance between overestimating the weight of a small cardboard box and overestimating the significance of a piece of evidence in a murder trial may seem great, but it is in fact a continuous path without clear boundaries. If twelve jurors were arranged according to their suggestibility, from the most resistant to the most impressionable, they would likely stand in the same order if tested for perceptual errors with these boxes.

The test can be simplified further. I have sometimes shown subjects pairs of circles drawn on paper and asked them to decide which circle in each pair was larger. The circles were always identical in size, but different numbers were printed at their centers. Suggestible individuals tend to judge the circle containing the number 79 as larger than the one containing 32. The same tendency appears in daily life when people assume the more attractive person to be more intelligent or the wealthier individual to be more capable.

What, then, does the psychologist mean by suggestion? From the outset, it must be clear that suggestion is neither abnormal nor pathological. The examples already given show that ordinary life and extreme disturbance meet here on a continuous scale. The woman who drafted her extravagant will had certainly passed beyond normal limits; the voter swayed by a parade or the customer captivated by sensational bargains is equally under suggestion, yet may be otherwise entirely normal. Suggestion is not a sign of weakness, nor would life be healthier if it were free from suggestive influence. On the contrary, without suggestion life would be colorless, lacking enthusiasm and conviction. Education, art, politics, and religion all rely upon it. Suggestion is simply any idea that takes hold of consciousness with such force that it inhibits and excludes competing ideas.

But what is meant by competing ideas? Consciousness can contain many thoughts at once, peacefully coexisting. We can think of black and white, summer and winter, man and woman, without conflict. When psychologists speak of opposing ideas, they refer not to thoughts themselves but to the attitudes they demand. I can think of a man and of a woman, but I cannot adopt simultaneously the attitude of treating the same person as both. I can think of summer and winter, but I must believe the season to be one or the other and act accordingly. The conflict lies in action, not in abstract thought. When we say that one idea excludes another, we mean that the attitude required by one excludes the attitude required by its opposite.

In ordinary life, free from overpowering suggestion, no idea enjoys special privilege. Each has its chance. A new idea may enter consciousness—from conversation, reading, or imagination—and encounter resistance from existing memories and associations. A fair contest follows, in which either the new or the old may prevail. Both cannot endure together, because we cannot perform contradictory actions at the same time. We cannot turn right and left simultaneously, open and close the hand at once, speak and remain silent. Suggestion intervenes precisely at this point: it prematurely decides the contest, suppressing alternatives and forcing the mind into a single, and sometimes dangerously narrow, course.

Erroneous ideas and inappropriate propositions enter our consciousness continually. Under ordinary conditions, they are immediately rejected through the corrective influence of opposing ideas supported by reliable memory and sound reasoning. The idea that is most firmly connected with the totality of our past experience is the one that survives. Each competing idea is reinforced by its own network of associations and must stand or fall on its own merits.

Whenever this balance is disturbed—whenever one idea, whether new or old, gains an unfair advantage so that opposing ideas are weakened or suppressed from the outset—we speak of *suggestion*. All prejudices and all firm convictions operate in this way. They deny opposing attitudes the opportunity to be tested. Such suggestive power may serve noble or destructive ends alike. A moral principle and a vicious impulse can each be strengthened by suggestion, for both may exclude the rival idea from the very beginning.

We call the readiness to receive such influences from others *suggestibility*. Its degree varies widely from person to person and fluctuates within the same individual from mood to mood, from hour to hour. Hypnotism represents only an artificially intensified state of suggestibility. Yet there are no sharp boundaries. Even the most obstinate mind is receptive to certain suggestions, and even the most deeply hypnotized person retains the capacity to resist ideas that violate the deepest principles of his life. Emotion invariably heightens suggestibility, as do fatigue and nervous exhaustion.

There is nothing mysterious in this process. Modern psychology understands it as a function of brain mechanism. Each idea corresponds to patterns of sensation accompanied by nervous excitation in sensory brain cells stimulated by the sense organs. But this excitation does not end in the sensory centers. It continues into motor pathways leading ultimately to the muscular system. The brain thus serves as an immense automatic switchboard, transmitting incoming sensory stimuli into outgoing motor impulses. Millions of pathways converge upon the brain, and millions lead outward again.

This fact alone would suggest that every sensory idea must result in action. Yet further observations clarify the mechanism. First, the motor pathways are so organized that when excitation runs strongly along one path, the pathways leading to an opposite action are inhibited.

When the impulse activates the nerves that open the hand, the channels that would clench the fist are simultaneously blocked. Second, ideas become vivid only when their channels of motor discharge are open. When those channels are closed, the corresponding ideas are suppressed and remain dim or entirely absent from consciousness.

A suggestion, then, is an idea whose sensory accompaniment keeps certain motor channels open while the channels leading to opposing actions are closed. Because these opposing channels are closed, the ideas associated with them are excluded from consciousness from the very beginning. If someone were to tell me, here in my library, "This is a garden," and if that statement acted as a suggestion, it would not paralyze all activity. I might continue reading, conversing, or recalling earlier events. But all activity would have to remain consistent with the attitude that this room is a garden. The impulse to take a book from the shelf would be inhibited; the books themselves would become, as it were, invisible. Instead, I should believe I saw flowers and feel inclined to pick them.

To accept my library shelves as flower beds would require an extreme degree of suggestibility, such as we associate with hypnosis. To mistake the trunk of a willow tree at twilight for a burglar requires far less suggestibility. To believe sensational headlines merely because they are printed in large type, despite a hundred past experiences that should awaken skepticism, requires still less.

If suggestion involves no mystery and no disease—if it rests on automatic opening and closing of motor channels largely independent of conscious will—and if every person is susceptible to suggestion while suggestion itself can invert truth and falsehood, then it is astonishing that courts of justice operate without systematic consultation of the psychologist and without drawing upon the insights offered by modern research on suggestion.

There is no participant in the judicial process who is immune. The defendant may have acted under suggestion at the time of the offense. Witnesses may have been influenced during their observation of events or may fall under suggestion while testifying. Even when their perception and memory are accurate, their narration may still be subtly distorted. Are lawyers, judges, or jurors exempt from such influences? Popular imagination readily suspects hypnotic influence behind crimes, yet this notion belongs more to sensational fiction than to serious legal analysis. Hypnotism is simply the most extreme form of suggestibility. For justice, it is far more important to recognize that milder states of suggestibility constitute the real breeding ground of impulsive and misguided actions.

We now know, for example, that alcohol intoxication can produce a state of suggestibility in which behavior closely resembling post-hypnotic obedience may occur. An instruction given impressively while alcohol has paralyzed the inhibitory centers may later be carried out in sobriety. Emotion exerts a similar effect. During panic, suggestibility may rise to such a degree that resistance collapses entirely. Mere membership in a crowd is often sufficient to weaken counteracting judgment. There are also individuals whose heightened suggestibility renders them perpetually vulnerable to chance influences. They are convinced by the last argument they hear, only to be persuaded just as fully by its opposite moments later.

Psychological experimentation can measure this constitutional susceptibility with precision. To ignore such nervous dispositions when judging criminal behavior is, in principle, no different from treating the mentally ill as if they were fully responsible. Justice cannot afford such blindness.

Even more critical than the influence of suggestion on the commission of a crime is its influence on the testimony of the witness. Distortion may begin at the very first stage—with perception itself. Whenever a court doubts whether a witness truly observed the facts correctly, we usually hear vague generalities about the likelihood of accurate judgment. Here, however, the first requirement should be to determine the *personal equation* of the observer and to establish, by scientific means, to what extent his perceptive consciousness is independent of intrusive suggestion.

A highly suggestible witness may hear distinct words where an objective observer heard nothing more than an indistinct noise. The difference may be decisive for the outcome of a trial. Words perceived by an unsuggestible mind may carry great evidential weight; the same words reported by a highly suggestible observer may be almost worthless.

To decide which is which, it should not be considered sufficient to rely on anecdote, intuition, or reputation.

With the tools of experimental psychology available, the degree of suggestibility can be determined with the same scientific precision that experts apply when deciding whether a bullet could have taken one path rather than another through the body.

Even where perception was reasonably accurate, recollection may later be profoundly distorted by suggestive side influences. Experiments have already shown the powerful effect of suggestive questioning. Beyond this, the entire atmosphere of the courtroom intensifies suggestibility. In widely discussed cases, circulating rumors—and above all the press—play a decisive role in reshaping memory. Recollections are unconsciously molded and reorganized.

An imaginative idea that fits a prejudice, a theory, or a suspicion may at first encounter resistance from genuine memory, but gradually it gains strength.

As soon as suggestibility increases, the fair contest between opposing ideas ceases; the rival memory is suppressed and finally extinguished.

Simple psychological tests could readily reveal such a change in mental condition. When a semi-hypnotic state of heightened suggestibility has set in, it is no wiser to keep a witness on the stand than it would be to examine him after he had consumed a bottle of whiskey.

And even when memory itself remains accurate, the *narration* may still be governed by suggestive forces. The reported story can then work backward through auto-suggestion, reshaping memory itself. Many people eventually come to believe their own exaggerated accounts after repeating them often enough.

It hardly needs emphasis that the most dangerously suggestible person in the courtroom may be neither the defendant nor the witness, but the juror.

His task demands freedom from suggestion more than almost any other mental quality. He must weigh conflicting evidence impartially. Psychological experiments demonstrate how easily this delicate balance can be disturbed when suggestibility is high. The experienced lawyer, guided by instinctive knowledge of the average juror, makes full use of psychological devices that bring one set of arguments vividly into the foreground while suppressing the force of opposing considerations.

Yet there exists a degree of suggestibility that completely defeats the ends of justice, and only psychological examination can expose such a deficiency.

A jury verdict becomes a caricature when insignificant or accidental circumstances, rather than evidence, determine the attitude of a suggestible juror.

Public opinion itself, driven by crowd instincts, is often the most suggestible judge of all. I once heard, at the center of political discussion, that after the Spanish War—when the nation was jubilant over the navy and numerous scandals seemed to implicate the army—Congress might never have voted such generous appropriations for the army had not West Point defeated Annapolis in a football match that year, thereby shifting suggestible public sentiment from navy to army. But when the court of public opinion weighs evidence, we are no longer dealing with law, but with politics. And it may be unwise to ask too closely how much suggestion operates in politics, for we might soon be confronted with the unsettling counter-question: is there anything in politics that is not suggestion?

Chapter of the End

Chapter–7.
Hypnotism and Its Legal Significance

William James argues that human testimony, even when honest and confident, can still contain serious errors. He suggests that mistakes may quietly enter the system of justice because people naturally believe their own perceptions. Although judges and juries carefully examine evidence, not every statement is completely reliable, as contradictions and misunderstandings often occur.

Those who once stubbornly denied the very existence of hypnotism have, by now, largely disappeared; their position was no more tenable than a refusal to acknowledge the reality of mental illness. At the opposite extreme stood those who regarded the hypnotic state as a mystical revelation, a gateway through which superhuman powers revealed themselves. They too have gradually lost their footing, for hypnotism is no more a supernatural mystery than sleep, hysteria, or epilepsy. Contemporary science understands hypnotic phenomena as entirely natural functions of mental life, closely related on one side to intense concentration, vivid imagination, and compliant volition, and on the other to sleep, dreaming, and certain forms of mental disturbance.

Much, of course, remains under active discussion. There is still no complete agreement as to where hypnotism ends and ordinary suggestion begins. Competing interpretations exist regarding the underlying brain processes, the special dispositions required for hypnosis, and even the precise nature of its symptoms. Yet on two points there is broad consensus. First, hypnotism is not without serious consequences and is therefore not a harmless diversion. Second, when applied by an experienced physician, it is a highly effective therapeutic instrument for many nervous and mental disorders. It has restored health, and with health a measure of happiness, to countless sufferers, and for that reason it has secured a permanent place in medical practice.

If hypnotism is here to stay, it is natural—and not without anxiety—that the question should arise: what is its relation to law and the courts, to crime and criminal procedure? The uncanny impression of one will exerting power over another invites the fear of dangerous social entanglements, while at the same time it suggests the possibility of new and potent tools in the service of justice. Imagination finds free play here. Popular fiction has made lavish use of hypnotism as a convenient device for criminal marvels, and the daily press has too often reported hypnotic crimes without any clear distinction between what is psychologically possible and what is pure fantasy. There is little guidance for the public, and it may therefore be useful to survey the entire field in which hypnotism and crime actually—or supposedly—intersect.

Public curiosity turns first to the question of whether the courts themselves might employ hypnotism as a means of uncovering hidden truth. Unsolicited letters on this topic arrive in abundance in a psychologist's correspondence, and it is precisely this proposal that seems to preoccupy the largest number of amateur criminologists. They follow murder trials with intense interest and often reach a state of genuine torment when uncertainty remains as to guilt, even after all evidence has been presented and a verdict rendered. Their uneasiness, they believe, could be resolved only by absolute certainty—by knowing beyond doubt who is telling the truth. Hypnotism, they argue, has the power to break down resistance of the will; if a witness were hypnotised and commanded to speak the truth, deception would become impossible. The idea appears simple and irresistibly promising.

From a strictly psychological standpoint, such a method might indeed succeed. In principle, it differs little from the involuntary confessions sometimes elicited from patients under hypnosis. I recall a student whom I was treating for cocaine addiction. He vehemently assured me, while fully awake, that he no longer possessed any cocaine. A few minutes later, under hypnosis, he accurately described the hiding place where it was concealed. Yet the practical difficulties begin at precisely the point most often misunderstood: no person can be hypnotised for the first time against his will by a stranger. A criminal who refuses to confess while fully conscious will not submit to hypnosis at the command of an outsider. Hypnosis does not operate like a chloroform-soaked sponge forcibly held to the mouth; if the subject's imagination does not cooperate in reaching the somnambulic state, no mesmerist can inject a mysterious fluid into his system.

Even if, by some improbable circumstance, hypnotisation were achieved, the result would not satisfy the requirements of justice. The hypnotised witness would no longer be in full possession of his mental faculties. The very essence of hypnosis lies in the inhibition of large portions of inner life: everything that might oppose the hypnotist's suggestion is suppressed. The person on the witness stand would thus cease, in a legal sense, to be the same individual who previously took the oath. His testimony would resemble, in principle, the disordered speech of a paranoiac. The unity of the legal personality would be broken.

A different situation arises when hypnosis is used to revive memories formed during an earlier hypnotic state. It is well established that a person may awaken from hypnosis with no recollection of what was said or experienced, yet recall everything clearly—even months later—once hypnosis is induced again. This sharpened dream-memory can, in certain cases, be of practical importance.

Here, the interruption of personal continuity presents less difficulty, since the aim is objective information.

For such purposes even an insane person may sometimes provide reliable evidence, for example regarding the location of hidden stolen goods.

Still, the direct use of hypnosis by a court would necessarily remain an extraordinary exception. Far more deserving of attention is the opposite case: the criminal who employs hypnotism. Here, too, popular misunderstanding abounds. Foremost among these misconceptions is the fear of the man endowed with paralysing powers—the figure who enters a room, fixes his gaze upon you, and renders you helpless; you hand over your jewels and the key to your safe, smiling helplessly while he calmly robs you. English newspapers once insisted that such a "burglar with the hypnotic eye" was "the latest product of America." *Punch* delighted in the theme, lampooning the imaginary John P. Beck of Fortieth Street, "as smart a burglar as one could meet," whose sole weapon was "the power of his black hypnotic eye." In the satire, witnesses became incoherent at his glance, judges lost their wits, and the trial ended with the judge declaring himself the criminal.

The caricature is amusing, but the accompanying seriousness was misplaced. *Punch* introduced the burlesque with the assertion that "Professor Münsterberg of Harvard and other learned men have set themselves to show that hypnotic power may become a most dangerous asset of the criminal."

The irony lies in the fact that few psychologists have been more persistent than I in ridiculing the belief in a special, mysterious "hypnotic power."

I am well aware that some colleagues disagree, but I have always maintained—and continue to maintain—that, in principle, anyone can hypnotise anyone.

Naturally, whoever undertakes to hypnotise—and in practice this should be only a physician—must master the technique and apply it with patience and skill. Individual differences undoubtedly exist. Not everyone can be deeply hypnotised; in many, the inhibition extends no further than an inability to open the eyes, while only about one in four experiences vivid hypnotic hallucinations.

Moreover, not everyone possesses the personal qualities that inspire the confidence and calm essential to guiding another into the hypnotic state. Voice, manner, gesture, phrasing, and general bearing may render certain individuals ineffective hypnotisers, however well they understand the procedure.

Yet in principle, hypnotising and being hypnotised are universal human capacities.

No special occult gift is required—no more than is required for falling in love or awakening love in another. The processes are human, natural, and intelligible, and precisely for that reason they demand sober understanding rather than superstition, especially when questions of crime and justice are at stake.

Yet, although every person may in principle exert hypnotic influence, no one can do so by a mere glance.

All tales of a secret power by which one individual's will seizes control of another's mind belong to the remnants of outdated mesmeric theories. Contemporary science has made it clear that everything depends on the attention and imagination of the hypnotised individual; no mysterious fluid flows from one person to another.

This mystical conception, born of unscientific superstition, reached its extreme in the widespread belief that a person might exercise such influence from a great distance, without the victim even knowing the source of the uncanny distortion of thought. Under such a fantasy, every heinous crime could be committed unseen, the distant hypnotiser inflicting suffering on an enemy or misusing innocent people as instruments of criminal designs.

This revival of witchcraft-like superstition is especially characteristic of minds that hover on the borderland between the normal and the abnormal.

An unsound intellect readily interprets stray impulses of its own mind as the intrusion of a distant adversary. In Germany, for example, a talented writer once inundated legislative bodies with pamphlets demanding new laws to punish those who, he claimed, produced criminal perversions through telepathic influence. Mental hospitals are filled with such ideas. Paranoiac patients are particularly inclined to explain their inner disturbances by the newest sensational agencies of their time: yesterday it was magnetism, today it may be X-rays, wireless telegraphy, or hypnotic influence from afar. In this country, students of Christian Science have become familiar with similar accusations. In *Science and Health,* Mrs. Eddy wrote: "In coming years the person or mind that hates his neighbour will have no need to traverse his fields, to destroy his flocks and herds ... for the evil mind will do this through mesmerism; and not in propria persona be seen committing the deed." Elsewhere she declared: "The secret mental assassin stalks abroad and needs to be branded to be known in what he is doing," and again: "That malicious animal-power seeks to kill his fellow mortals, morally and physically, and then to charge the innocent with his crimes."

There should be no compromise on this point. The doctrine of so-called "Malicious Animal Magnetism" is a complete distortion of the facts and morally ruinous in its implications. Nothing of the kind is ever possible.

Some argue that if the surprising phenomena of hypnotism are real, then telepathic mesmerism might also be possible, since the effects appear similar. This reasoning is no sounder than arguing that, because a hen can hatch from a hen's egg, it might just as well emerge from a white candy egg because the two look alike. The essential conditions of hypnotism and telepathy are fundamentally different and cannot be compared: the latter would indeed be a mystery, while the former is no more difficult to explain than any ordinary act of perception and attention.

There is, of course, no reason to deny that a person may fall into a hypnotic state while the hypnotiser is at another place. The condition is simply that the subject must previously have been hypnotised by that person and that his own imagination has become bound to the thought of the absent hypnotiser. I myself have repeatedly induced hypnosis by telephone or even by letter. I once treated a morphine addict who initially came daily to my laboratory to be hypnotised; later it was sufficient to say over the telephone, "Take out your watch; in two minutes you will fall asleep," or to write, "As soon as you have read this note, you will be in the hypnotic state." In this sense I exercised an influence at a distance, but it was not my will-power that acted; it was the patient's own imagination. At the moment he read my letter in his suburb and fell asleep, I was not thinking of him at all. Such effects by correspondence would, of course, have been impossible had they not been preceded by repeated hypnotisation in personal contact.

Even that degree of preparation may not be necessary when not full hypnosis but only suggestive influence is involved. Recently I received a letter from a woman in the South whose son suffered from morphine addiction. I had never seen either of them. She wrote: "My son has been impressed with the belief that your treatment is all he needs to be cured. In a dream, he said, you stood before him with the fingertips of your hands trembling and said, 'I have the power to influence your will.' He woke repeating, 'You have the power to control my will.'

That morning he forgot to take the morphine at the usual time and soon went down to the beach without his morphine outfit in his pocket—an unusual thing." He himself was convinced that my will was acting upon him, although I did not even know of his existence.

The decisive factor in all such cases is confidence. Anyone who has witnessed the hypnotic effects produced by the great master of hypnotism, Professor Bernheim of Nancy, moving from bed to bed in the clinic and merely saying, "Sleep, sleep," might well believe that no one else could attain such influence. Yet this was not because he possessed a special power; the essential point was that the entire population around Nancy approached him with an extraordinary tension of expectancy and trust. I recall a woman who suffered from nervous complaints and whom I at first could not hypnotise at all. I felt an inner resistance and eventually discovered its cause. She had consulted so many physicians who sent her large bills that she believed doctors humbug nervous patients for money. I explained that, as a psychologist, I undertook such work purely in the interest of science and had never accepted payment from any patient. Two minutes later she was in deep hypnotic sleep. The subject's attention and emotional attitude thus matter far more than any supposed power of the hypnotiser.

This does not exclude the possibility that attention and emotion may be stirred intentionally, even maliciously, without the conscious awareness of the person affected. No special power is required to awaken love, yet a coquettish smile from a wilful girl may disturb the peace of any man.

In a similar way, a hypnotiser need not wait until the subject lies down with the conscious expectation of being hypnotised; he may work slowly and systematically, through countless small influences, upon the imagination of a susceptible person. While the notion of a hypnotic eye that fascinates at a single glance and the fantasy of malicious magnetism from a distance are both absurd, the gradual and persistent gaining of influence over an unresisting mind is certainly possible.

Such influence rarely culminates in a full hypnotic state. Instead, it merges imperceptibly into the forms of submission and suggestibility that belong to ordinary social life. There is heightened openness to influence in love and fear, in the pupil's attitude toward the teacher, and in the patient's trust in the physician. Nowhere is there a sharp dividing line between these valuable forms of social authority and the abnormal suggestions that reach their climax in complete hypnosis.

These semi-hypnotic states can, of course, serve the good, but the dangers of their misuse are equally evident and demand serious consideration wherever law, responsibility, and justice are concerned.

I recall the tragic case of a young woman from the American West who appears to have lived for years in a state of partial depersonalisation. She had completed her college education and advanced university studies, and every instructor and fellow student spoke of her with admiration. She was a woman of rare charm and refinement. Yet her most beautiful qualities revealed themselves in her family life. Her elderly mother and her sisters were the centre of her thoughts, her devotion to them unwavering and tender.

The family later made the acquaintance of an Italian who presented himself as a wealthy count. In reality, he was destitute, uneducated, vulgar, and without any trace of refinement, belonging to the lowest social level. The young woman felt an immediate and profound disgust toward him. Nevertheless, he contrived to see her repeatedly. She became painfully aware of his growing influence over her. She sensed it with aversion; she felt a physical shudder when he looked at her. And yet, despite her repulsion, an uncanny fascination seized her—a strange and overpowering attraction that she could neither understand nor resist. Against her will, she felt compelled to do what he asked, and eventually what he commanded.

She despised him, and yet one day they secretly left the house and were married. Immediately afterward, he took possession of her considerable property.

But his control did not end there. Under his influence she initiated absurd and malicious lawsuits designed to deprive her own family of everything they owned. She appeared in court and, under oath, uttered the most cruel accusations against her mother—a woman who had never ceased to love her daughter with complete devotion. Everyone who had known her before felt, from her expression and her voice, that she was no longer herself, but merely the passive instrument of a ruthless and calculating schemer.

Her mother said in despair: "Sometimes, for a few minutes, I felt as though I could reach her—then she would be gone again, miles and miles away. There are no words to describe the horror of it." And her sister wrote: "I should go mad if I had to see her often." Such a spectacle—a mind that is still recognisably the old personality and yet profoundly altered—is not altogether rare in our courtrooms. It represents a hypnotic or semi-hypnotic condition laden with grave social danger. Yet, as emphasised earlier, there is no reason to fear that such a state can arise suddenly or be imposed from a distance. It requires persistent influence, acts primarily upon neurotic individuals with a special disposition toward mental inhibition, and never attains the depth of complete hypnosis.

The next question is how far full hypnosis itself belongs within the sphere of criminal action. One possibility immediately presents itself: a hypnotised person may become the powerless instrument of the hypnotiser's criminal will. He may pull the trigger, mix poison into food, steal, or forge documents, while the true and responsible agent is not the one who commits the act, but the one who directed it through hypnotic suggestion. Such phenomena have been demonstrated countless times in experimental settings.

I may, for example, tell a hypnotised subject that he is to poison a visitor whom I shall call in from the next room. I prepare a harmless sugar powder and assure him that it is arsenic. I dissolve it before his eyes in a glass of water and then summon a colleague. The hypnotised subject takes the glass and offers it to the visitor. One sees his hesitation, perhaps even trembling, but at last he overcomes his resistance and hands over the liquid which he believes to be deadly poison. The apparent danger of such secret crimes seems even greater when we consider post-hypnotic suggestion.

In practical life, the opportunity to commit a crime during the hypnotic trance itself is rare. But the hypnotiser may order the act to be carried out hours or days after awakening. Every experimenter knows how easily a subject can be induced to perform an absurd action long after the hypnotic session has ended. "This afternoon at four o'clock, go to your friend, stand on one leg, and recite the alphabet." Such a command will be carried out with remarkable precision. The subject will not anticipate it beforehand; but when the appointed time arrives, he experiences an irresistible impulse to go to his friend's house and act as instructed. He will carry it out with a feeling of freedom and will invent some illogical explanation to justify his behaviour to himself. He recites the alphabet, he tells himself, because his friend once misspelled a word.

Theoretically, one might ask whether he could not just as well be ordered to run to his friend's house and shoot him. He would again feel himself acting freely and would again invent a motive. The picture becomes still more sinister if the hypnotiser adds the further suggestion that no one else will ever be able to hypnotise him again and that he will completely forget that he was ever hypnotised. Experiments show that such post-hypnotic effects are, in principle, possible. It is therefore not surprising that literature has made abundant use of post-hypnotic suggestion as a convenient device for secret murder, just as it did for the miraculous singing of Trilby.

And yet, in the face of all this, I must make a confession of my own. I have serious doubts about the purity of Trilby's hypnotic artistry, and far more than doubts when it comes to hypnotic murder. Indeed, I am practically convinced that no genuine murder has ever been committed by an innocent person solely under the influence of post-hypnotic suggestion. I have seen men kill with paper daggers, poison with harmless flour, and shoot with unloaded revolvers in laboratories and clinics, under the watchful eyes of physicians. But I have never been persuaded that, in these demonstrations, there was not always a background awareness of artificiality in the subject's mind—an awareness that would not exist in real life and that would not overcome the moral resistance which stands firm outside the experimental setting. Absolute proof is, of course, impossible, since we cannot kill for the sake of experiment.

It may be argued that courts have already condemned men for murders in which they were merely passive instruments of another's hypnotic influence. Yet no authenticated murder case is known in which such a theory remained plausible after all evidence was considered.

Lawyers have repeatedly asked me whether a defence based on hypnosis or post-hypnotic suggestion could stand. My answer has always been the same: despite experimental appearances to the contrary, hypnotic suggestion does not seem capable of breaking down the deepest inner resistance. From this standpoint, there is no real danger to justice.

The frequent claim by defendants that they must have been hypnotised is, however, seldom a deliberate fabrication. More often it reflects the experience of the unbalanced or diseased mind, in which criminal impulses arise as though they were foreign intruders, seizing the personality without conscious deliberation or free choice of motive. In such cases, the sufferer interprets his own incomprehensible actions sincerely, though erroneously, as the product of some strange external influence.

Yet there is another aspect, and it would be reckless to ignore the distinction it demands.

You cannot compel an honest person to steal or to kill; but you *can* induce him to perform actions that are not immoral in themselves and yet possess a criminal character.

A scoundrel, for instance, may give a post-hypnotic suggestion that his subject—a man of independent means and without close relatives—should visit a lawyer and deposit a last will leaving all his property to the hypnotiser. Here no resistance of moral principle is involved. The man who gives away all that he owns follows the command because the impulse encounters no barrier in the habits of a trained conscience.

We may go one step further, and this step is by no means impossible. The hypnotiser may add the post-hypnotic suggestion of suicide. The following day the victim is found dead in his room. Everything indicates self-destruction; no suspicion arises. The hypnotiser, by virtue of the spurious will, becomes the heir. Such cases have been reported, and they are not intrinsically improbable. The ease with which a hypnotiser may conceal the traces of his crime through carefully planted suggestions makes the danger all the greater.

To this group belong also post-hypnotic perjuries. If a witness knew that he was swearing falsely, his moral convictions would revolt, just as they would in the case of theft or murder. But here he believes what he swears.

On his side there is no conscious crime, only confusion of ideas and falsified memory. The crime lies wholly with the one who fabricated the artificial delusion. In many such cases the hypnotised subject is an active sufferer—he commits the act and suffers its consequences. These cases are often accompanied by others in which the subject is a passive victim.

French literature on hypnotism abounds with reports of hypnotised women who became victims of sexual crimes. No warning can be too emphatic against hypnotisation by anyone except trustworthy and responsible physicians. Other cases concern simple fraud.

A post-hypnotic suggestion may induce one person to pay the price of genuine pearls for glass beads, or compel another to purchase a house entirely useless for his needs.

A physician trained in scientific psychology will have little difficulty in assisting the court in such situations and in arriving at a correct diagnosis. Without thorough experience in psychology, however, no one—physician or layman—will be able to disentangle these cases. The hypnotiser may have suggested complete forgetfulness and may even have prohibited any further hypnotisation; yet there always remains some small opening through which the psychologist can insert a wedge and ultimately break open the entire mental structure. It should be added that the psychologist has no difficulty in detecting any simulation of hypnotic states.

There remains one further and important relation between hypnotism and crime: hypnotisation may prevent crime. Our moral interest in suppressing criminal impulses inclines us to draw a sharp boundary between socially destructive tendencies and impulses that are morally indifferent. Psychologically, however, such a clear line cannot be acknowledged.

The craving for an immoral or illegal act may take hold of a weak nervous system in the same way as any neurasthenic impulse, and it is therefore not unjustified to hope that criminal dispositions may find the same relief through hypnotic treatment as other nervous disturbances.

Last year, within the same week, two young people approached me with almost identical complaints: they could not control their ideas and desires. One suffered from the impulse to kill certain persons; whenever he encountered them, he felt an overwhelming urge to strike them down.

The other suffered from the impulse to shift her gaze constantly from one eye to the other of anyone with whom she spoke. The impulse to kill was potentially of the gravest consequence; the impulse to move the eyes was, in itself, utterly harmless. Yet the second patient was the greater sufferer.

She had once noticed, by chance, a striking difference in colour between a man's eyes.

This led her to look alternately at one eye and then the other. What began as a trivial observation became a habit stronger than her will. By the time she came to me, the compulsion had grown so oppressive that she contemplated suicide because life had become intolerable under this incessant urge to swing her gaze back and forth.

I treated the dangerous homicidal impulse and the harmless ocular impulse in exactly the same manner—by inhibitory suggestion—and both disappeared under hypnotic treatment in the same length of time.

Yet it is evident that criminal impulses cannot simply be treated as a mere appendix to neurasthenic conditions. Here the most complex, and partly moral, questions arise. Have we the right to reinforce moral conduct by hypnotic means rather than by an appeal to spiritual and ethical energies? If we cure a morally depraved boy of his habit of stealing through hypnosis, would not the logical consequence be to entrust his entire education and upbringing to such a powerful and seemingly safe influence? At this point the discussion opens into the widest range of social problems.

We are thus led to a new and separate question—one of profound importance: What can the modern psychologist contribute to the prevention and suppression of crime?

Chapter of the End

Chapter–8. The Psychological Foundations of Crime Prevention

This chapter argues that no one is born a criminal; rather, crime develops when society weakens the mental balance between impulse and inhibition. Through examples such as drug addiction, mental deficiency, alcohol experiments, and environmental influence, the author shows that criminal behavior arises when strong impulses are not effectively checked by counter-ideas like moral training, social responsibility, and self-control.

A few weeks ago, a most pitiable human wreck wandered into my laboratory. At the first glance I saw how morphine had devastated the body of a man still in his prime. Trembling, with restless, rolling eyes, he confessed that he was consuming thirty grains of the destructive poison every day. He could neither eat nor sleep; he had not worked for years; he had abandoned wife and child. It was a gruesome story of prolonged misery. He had been sent to asylums without result; he remained the slave of his craving, and society had learned to treat him with contempt and disgust.

Slowly, piece by piece, I drew from him the full tragedy of his life. He had once been successful and industrious. Then came an accident, and he was taken to a hospital in the South. There, to secure restful nights, the surgeons administered morphine every evening—only a small injection, an eighth of a grain. When he left the hospital, his hip was healed, but his sleep was gone. He could not rest without the drug. Day by day the dose increased. He became a morphinist—an outcast, drained of energy and hope.

For weeks I have been combating this passion through persistent suggestive treatment. The dose he requires has now been reduced to a hundredth part of its former amount. His strength has slowly returned, and with it his enjoyment of life. He will soon be cured. Yet each day, as I devote my full energy to this task, I am forced to reflect on the cruelty with which society treated him. He was not born a "dope fiend." He did not choose the poison. Organized society injected it into his system—only a small dose, it is true, but enough to make the craving irresistible. And when that craving grew to ruinous proportions, society was ready to despise and condemn him. Even in the best case, it could offer only heroic efforts to overcome the gigantic passion it had itself recklessly awakened.

To me, this diseased craving is a symbol of crime everywhere. No one is born a criminal. But society administers, often without the individual's will, the first ruinous injection—again, a small one, an eighth of a grain—and then looks on with contempt as the implanted instinct grows. When it has destroyed the individual, society finally intervenes with police, courts, and punishment. Almost always, it is too late. To prevent that first reckless injection would have been better than all the labor of prisons and penitentiaries.

At last this conviction is gaining ground everywhere: the prevention of crime is more important than its punishment. It is claimed that this country spends annually hundreds of millions more on combating existing crime than on all its combined efforts in charity, education, and religion.

The feeling is growing that a fraction of this expenditure and energy would suffice to ensure that much habitual crime never comes into existence at all. For such a result, however, it is essential that all social forces work together in harmony, and that no science capable of contributing to this immense task withhold its aid. It is therefore the clear duty of modern experimental psychology to direct its serious attention to these problems, and the psychologist may rightly ask for a hearing.

Public opinion, however, often calls upon the psychologist for a very different purpose.

He is expected to relieve society of responsibility by testifying that the criminal is born as such. Reminiscences of earlier theories and schools have fostered the belief that the true scientist must accept the idea of the "born criminal," alongside other human abnormalities supposedly beyond social influence, such as epilepsy—or, on the brighter side of life, musical genius. In this form, however, the doctrine is misleading, and the psychologist must refuse to endorse it.

No one denies the importance of those investigations that examined the bodily and mental characteristics of prison populations, nor the value of anthropological, sociological, and psychological studies of their physical traits, habits, language, sensitivities, and emotions. Yet none of these results justify the conclusion that criminals are born as such. On the contrary, they strengthen the indictment of society itself.

From the outset, we must recognize how vague it is, psychologically, to speak of a "criminal disposition" as though it were a single, unified mental state. Earlier pseudo-sciences found it convenient to speak of distinct faculties—of morality, of architecture, of criminality—as though each were a simple function located in one corner of the brain. Such assumptions were necessary only because those theories sought physical signs for complex mental traits. Today we know that such traits arise from countless processes distributed across vast regions of the brain. We may localize simple sensations, but not entire perceptions, and still less complex patterns of thought, emotion, and will.

How, then, does the average person succeed in living an honest life? Impressions and thoughts constantly awaken ideas charged with pleasure or displeasure. Pleasurable ideas stir desire and impulse toward action; unpleasant ideas prompt avoidance. No separate act of will is required—the idea itself presses the inner button and movement follows. From the earliest moments of life, this mechanism governs behavior. But from the beginning, life complicates it. Before action occurs, the tempting idea is checked by another thought—perhaps of danger, harm, or consequence. The desire to reach for the fruit is countered by the knowledge that it is poisonous. One impulse urges the hand forward; the opposing impulse draws it back. The stronger idea prevails.

These counter-ideas may be social in nature—the fear of punishment or contempt—or they may be ethical or religious, effective even where no social sanction applies. In every case, the mechanism remains the same: action results from the struggle of ideas. There is no independent moral agent selecting among them; the ideas themselves, in their vividness, emotional tone, and attached impulses, constitute the working personality. A law-abiding life results when socially forbidden desires are consistently inhibited by stronger counter-ideas—fear of harm, respect for law, or moral dignity.

From a psychological standpoint, there is therefore no special faculty of non-criminal behavior. It overlaps entirely with the general capacity to live prudently and cautiously. By imperceptible steps, avoidance of physical danger leads to avoidance of social danger and thus to lawful conduct. There is no sharp dividing line. One person may obey the law out of fear of detection, another out of moral conviction, yet both appear equally blameless in the eyes of the law. Criminality cannot be reduced to a single formula.

A decent life requires that any idea stimulating forbidden action simultaneously awakens opposing ideas that inhibit it—

and that these opposing ideas prevail. Crime may result if these counter-ideas were never learned, or arise too slowly, or are too weak; or if the original impulse is too strong, its emotion too intense, or the inhibitory mechanism itself defective.

A disturbance at any point in this complex process may lead to conflict with the law. And yet how different are these cases in nature. Where, then, is the boundary at which a defect becomes abnormal? Strong impulses may be harmless if restraint is equally strong; weak restraint may suffice if temptation is slight. The problem admits no simple division, and it is precisely here that psychology must guide any serious effort at the prevention of crime.

Moreover, it is evident that none of these defects operates exclusively in the direction of crime. A brain in which counter-ideas arise too slowly does not suffer merely in matters of legal conduct; the deficiency is general. Ideas come sluggishly, mental outlook is narrow, and the individual appears dull and mentally inert. Likewise, a brain in which opposing ideas fail to inhibit impulses will behave recklessly in every sphere of life; such a person runs risks indiscriminately and shows little concern for consequences.

And where impulses are excessively strong, the resulting lack of balance manifests itself emotionally in all domains.

In short, there are minds that are slow, stupid, brutal, excitable, lazy, eccentric, reckless, or dull—and in every such mind there exists a certain increased probability of conflict with the law. Yet to be born with a mind whose special stupidity, carelessness, or vehemence gives crime an easier foothold than in the average case does not mean to be a born criminal. The world is full of poorly balanced or poorly associating minds. Nature has not equipped them generously for the struggle of social existence; they are less fit than others. But their possible end within prison walls is only one among many dangers that life holds for them. The same defective mental equipment may make them unable to gain a secure position, to form lasting friendships, or to protect themselves against disease. In brief, criminals are not born; rather, men are born with minds that work imperfectly.

And who shall say where the perfectly functioning mind begins? No brain works flawlessly. What intelligence, what temperament, would deserve to be called ideal? "All the world is peculiar." The difference is always one of degree.

This, indeed, is precisely the situation the psychologist encounters. If we turn to the professional criminal who has become a specialist in burglary, forgery, or theft, and whose life has been shaped by long years in penitentiaries, we find mental types that differ markedly from the average. But these differences are the result of training and environment. Such individuals have become almost incapable of avoiding crime; they continue their career because it has become their only possible path. Yet it was not an inborn disposition that forced them into burglary. If we abstract from the effects of such training in the social underworld, and from the influences of poor education, bad example, disease, and neglect, we find among criminals the same varieties of mind as elsewhere—only with a far higher proportion of mental inferiority: narrow and unintelligent minds, vehement and passionate minds, minds with weak comprehension, minds with deficient inhibitory power, minds lacking normal emotional balance, and minds without energy for sustained work.

When a school for delinquent boys was carefully examined, it was found that out of two hundred boys, one hundred and twenty-seven showed general deficiencies—either feeble-mindedness, hysterical emotionality, or epileptic disturbance.

The figures become still more illuminating when further facts are added. In eighty-five cases, one or both parents were drunkards; in twenty-four cases the parents were insane; in twenty-six cases epileptic; and in twenty-six more they suffered from other nervous diseases. The criminal tendency was not inherited by these children; what they inherited was an insufficient resistance and capacity of the central nervous system—an inheritance from abnormal and degenerate parents.

If we translate these facts into the language of experimental psychology, we may consult the careful tests conducted with female criminals in Southern penitentiaries and compare them with female students at a large university. Point by point, the results differ. In memory tests, the average student recalled a series of seven letters or eight numerals, while under identical conditions the average criminal recalled only five letters or six numerals. In tests of tactile discrimination, students distinguished two compass points on the right forearm at a distance of sixteen millimetres, while criminals required a distance of twenty-four millimetres. When pulling on a hook as rapidly as possible, the students' muscular energy declined by 1.6 pounds in half a minute, while that of the criminals declined by 2.4 pounds. When given a word as a stimulus for free association, the average student produced ten associations per minute, the average criminal only five. In every respect, the criminal average reveals poorer mental equipment than the carefully selected student average.

Yet here again, no single feature points to a special destiny toward crime. Criminals are recruited largely from the mentally inferior—that is the sole kernel of truth in the doctrine of the born criminal. But mental inferiority, whether intellectual, emotional, or volitional, does not compel a person to steal or to burglarize. Such a person may never rival the clever, well-balanced, energetic individual, but society can still provide a modest, humble, yet secure place even for the most unintelligent, indifferent, or unenergetic. No one is predestined by the structure of his brain to end his life in the penitentiary.

It may be objected that there are cases in which crime arises from irresistible impulse, from total lack of inhibition, or from other defects that exclude free self-determination. But in such cases we no longer have the right to speak of crime; we are dealing with insanity. A man who sets fires because he hallucinates the voice of God commanding him to burn a town is not a criminal. Moreover, the pathological impulses of a diseased mind are not confined to criminal acts. Crime is merely one possible outcome; the disturbance itself is general. The same irresistible impulse may be directed against the individual's own body and lead to self-mutilation or suicide.

This holds true even for milder cases. Only today I examined an eleven-year-old boy who was brought to me because he had been caught stealing from time to time. He was a gentle child, raised amid comfort and the best, most loving influences. He struggles earnestly against his impulse and speaks of it openly. At times it comes upon him like an attack; he longs for money, perhaps to buy firecrackers, and cannot resist until the act is done. He told me, with tears, that afterward he scarcely knows why he did it. Yet at first glance it was evident that the boy was not normally constituted, and that these episodes were pathological, akin to epileptic or hysterical seizures. To prevent such eruptions of a diseased brain is not the prevention of crime; it is, on the one hand, the treatment of disease, and on the other, the protection of society against dangerous patients.

In genuine crime, by contrast, we must assume that inhibition by counter-ideas would have been possible if sufficient mental energy had been mobilized. Crime, therefore, is not a disease, and there is no need to justify our prisons by treating them as asylums. Every action is, of course, the necessary outcome of preceding causes, but it remains a free and thus responsible act so long as those causes operate upon a mental mechanism capable of an unhampered interplay of influences. The insane or the hypnotized mind lacks such freedom and therefore cannot commit crime. The merely stupid, reckless, brutal, or indifferent mind, however, still possesses freedom—though the probability of disastrous outcomes is, for such minds, alarmingly high.

If, therefore, we exclude the pathological mind from further consideration, we may state with confidence that no one is born a criminal. The question then arises: what must society do to ensure that no one becomes a criminal? The youngest of the sciences, eugenics, looks backward and urges society to prevent the birth of mentally weak and inferior individuals altogether. Indeed, the darker pages of vital statistics reveal that an overwhelming proportion of degenerate personalities are the offspring of drunkards, epileptics, and the mentally diseased. Yet our most urgent deficiency lies elsewhere. We must take the world as it is: millions of minds, strong and weak, intelligent and dull, emotionally balanced and unstable, are born and released into the streets of our cities. What guidance can psychology offer so that their path does not lead from the street to the prison cell?

Here the problem becomes clearer and more manageable. We understand the mental mechanism that keeps individuals within the bounds of law, and we can therefore anticipate the influences that threaten it.

If lawful conduct depends upon the counter-idea balancing and overcoming the first impulse, then the likelihood of crime must increase whenever impulses are strengthened, counter-ideas weakened or eliminated, inhibitory control damaged, or the delicate balance otherwise disturbed. This is precisely the field in which experimental psychology can render service. In the laboratory, the psychologist can isolate individual factors and study their effects under controlled conditions.

Let us consider a few illustrations. Crime presupposes an impulse toward action that should normally be checked. The stronger the impulse, the harder it is to restrain.

The psychologist therefore asks: what conditions intensify impulses? Does imitation, for example, possess such power? Speculation alone cannot answer this, and even so-called practical experience may mislead. But laboratory experiment speaks in precise figures.

Suppose I ask my subjects to perform rhythmic finger movements that lift a weight, while an apparatus records the exact force of each contraction. After a time, the energy appears exhausted; the impulse can no longer raise the weight more than a few millimetres, and the curve sinks almost to zero. Encouraging words or sharp commands have some effect; the curve rises slightly, then quickly falls again. But when I myself perform the same rhythmic movement before the subject's eyes, the result changes dramatically. The curve rises with unexpected strength. The movement now follows an act of imitation, and this simple fact reinforces the impulse beyond anything the subject's unaided will could achieve. It is as though the observed action suddenly unlocks reserves of stored energy.

This experiment can be varied endlessly, yet the outcome remains the same.

The vivid demonstration of an act gives the imitative impulse its maximum force, and under such conditions inhibition becomes most difficult. From this single fact flow countless positive suggestions for education, training, and self-development. But still more urgent are the warnings it conveys. When millions of copies of sensational newspapers, filled with graphic portrayals of crime, enter the homes of suggestible readers, every latent impulse toward forbidden action is dangerously reinforced. Each brutal deed spreads outward, magnifying lawless tendencies in its surroundings. The abolition of prizefights and whipping posts is not enough if the daily press continues to glorify violence.

Consider another direction. Anything that weakens restraint must be fatal to fragile honesty. Here again psychological experiment can analyze the effects of our everyday stimulants—coffee and tea, tobacco and alcohol, drugs and nervines.

In the laboratory, the changes observed may appear small: a slight alteration in reaction speed, a minor decline in memory accuracy, a marginal impairment in discrimination. Yet when such effects are projected onto the scale of a modern metropolis, where millions live under constant artificial stimulation, their social significance becomes enormous.

Take the well-studied case of alcohol. Let us examine a group of normal individuals under ordinary conditions. We begin with reaction-time experiments, measuring in thousandths of a second how quickly a person responds to a flash of light or a sharp sound. We then introduce choice reactions, requiring discrimination between different stimuli. Next come memory tests, learning series of letters, numbers, or words. We may add simple arithmetic tasks, association experiments, measurements of muscular strength, judgments of space and time, imitation of rhythms, rapid counting, and tests of sustained attention. Each yields precise averages.

Now we repeat these tests after the ingestion of alcohol—after twenty minutes, an hour, or two hours, and after varying doses. Only through such comprehensive testing can we disentangle the true effects and determine where the disturbance lies. Some functions appear improved at first glance.

Reaction times, for instance, may shorten; a subject who normally requires 150 thousandths of a second to respond to a sound may need only 125 after a moderate dose.

But is this genuine improvement? The same records reveal that wrong reactions now appear—premature responses, impulsive movements triggered before the stimulus is fully perceived. Control is weakened; the impulse fires at the slightest provocation instead of waiting for conscious verification.

Here lies the danger. What appears as increased speed is often merely diminished restraint.

And diminished restraint, multiplied by millions and extended over daily life, creates precisely the conditions under which crime finds its opportunity. Psychology thus teaches us not only how crime occurs, but also how it may be prevented—by guarding the delicate balance between impulse and inhibition upon which lawful life depends.

In the same manner, dynamometric tests initially suggest that alcohol produces an improvement in motor energy. For a brief interval the muscles seem stronger, the effort more vigorous. Yet half an hour later the situation is reversed: muscular efficiency declines, and the apparent gain proves illusory. In the realm of mental associations, the emergence of new ideas becomes slower; thought is retarded. More significant still, the associative process itself grows mechanical. If we distinguish between *external* associations—where one idea calls forth another merely through contiguity in space or time—and *internal* associations—those grounded in meaning, purpose, and inner relation—we find that alcohol markedly increases the former while suppressing the latter. External links multiply; internal connections fade.

The disturbance becomes even more pronounced in mechanical memorisation, which at first is facilitated, and in calculation, which suffers almost immediately. The most conspicuous apparent improvement is seen in reading, while the greatest difficulty appears in intellectual integration and sustained reasoning. When these various threads are brought together through careful analysis, a unified picture emerges: motor reactions are made easier, acts of apperception are impaired, the interplay of ideas is weakened, inhibitions are reduced, superficial and mechanical connections dominate the mind, and intellectual processes become sluggish.

Is it necessary to demonstrate how each of these changes favours criminal behaviour? Counter-ideas arise too slowly; action follows the first impulse before it can be checked; inhibition of forbidden deeds loses its force; and the craving for rash, vehement movement becomes overwhelming. In this way experimental psychology transforms the vague impressions of casual observation into exact knowledge. It replaces prejudice with measurement, conjecture with demonstration, and emotion with evidence.

Moreover, these general conclusions can be refined through subtler inquiry. How does alcohol act in different climates and seasons, at different hours of the day, during work or fatigue, in health and illness, with food or without, in the young and the old, in men and women, across races and social conditions? How do the effects of pure alcohol compare with those of beer, wine, or spirits? Only by such differentiated experimental study can we hope to establish rational safeguards against one of the most persistent sources of social harm.

The same methods may be applied to tobacco, coffee, tea, bromides, morphine, and other drugs; but also to the effects of physical and mental overstrain, impure air and inadequate lighting, irrational nutrition and insufficient sleep, excessive sports and emotional exhaustion, and countless other factors woven into the daily life of the masses. Only upon such an experimental foundation can regulation and improvement be securely built. Mere prohibition may be easy in theory, but it is impracticable in the face of fatigue, poverty, and human need—and even where possible, it may be unwise. Psychology must indicate the middle path: one that closes the sources of evil without drying up the springs of vitality.

Indeed, simple abstinence from all stimulants is no true solution. It is the psychologist, more than anyone else, who recognises the dangers of monotony and emptiness; who understands that the craving for stimulation and excitement arises from deep conditions of human existence; and who knows that complete suppression often leads to mental explosions more destructive than the evils it seeks to prevent. Laboratory experiments can show how a dreary state of waiting and monotony alters mental balance: how certain functions starve while others become dangerously overstrained. A condition of dull expectancy emerges, in which the hunger for contrast intensifies desire until reaction becomes more violent than under any stimulant. Projected onto the masses, such a state breeds gambling, perversion, and irrational crimes—acts driven by imagination alone, undertaken to escape the emptiness of unstimulated life.

Experimental psychology may also examine the finer mechanisms of inhibition itself. To what extent does the suppression of motor impulse depend upon the strength of the counter-stimulus, and to what extent upon habit—upon the steady reinforcement that comes from repetition? How are these processes altered by interruptions in training or by the emotional tone of ideas? Simple reaction-time measurements, varied by the introduction of warning signals designed to counterbalance impulses, can yield illuminating results. Even the modest, schematic experiments of the laboratory reveal with clarity how a climate of lawlessness, corruption, and habitual disregard for authority undermines the inhibitory power of law and prepares the soil for a harvest of crime.

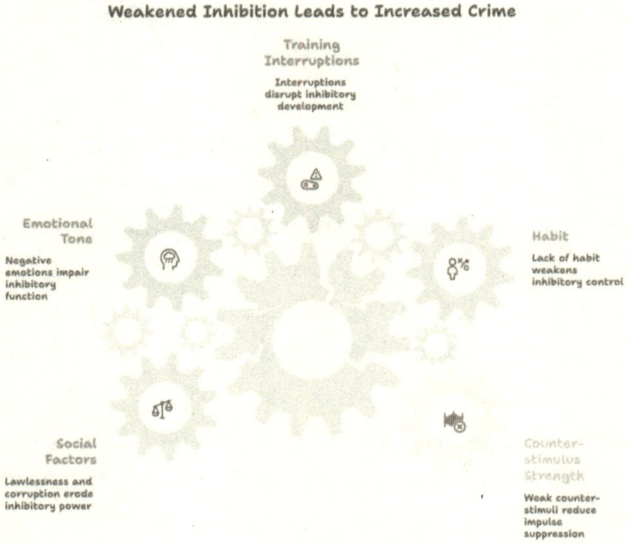

Here lies the unique strength of psychological experimentation: it dissects vast social movements within the smallest and simplest models of mental force.

From such precise analysis, the step toward prevention is short. What commercial excess, street vice, mass recklessness, sensational journalism, theatrical frivolity, and gambling excitement mean for the vulnerable individual can scarcely be understood more clearly than through these microscopic representations of the same forces at work.

In them, society may read both the sources of its dangers and the means of their control.

The psychologist, therefore, cannot accept the belief that the prevention of crime is achieved wholly—or even mainly—by the mere threat of punishment. The decisive question is not whether punishment satisfies a social demand for retaliation, nor whether it may indirectly contribute to reform by educating the man who is shut behind the doors of a penitentiary. The sole question here is whether the fear of future judicial punishment can operate as a sufficiently strong counter-idea to inhibit the criminal impulse at the critical moment. Psychological insight compels us to answer with grave doubt.

Too many conditions conspire to frustrate such an expectation. In the concrete situation, the hope of escaping justice often carries a stronger emotional tone than the abstract fear of a general law. The intensity of the forbidden desire narrows the field of consciousness and suppresses the idea of consequences. The dull mind fails to connect cause and effect; the slow mind brings the restraining idea too late, when the deed is already done; the vehement mind overwhelms the mechanisms of inhibition; the emotional mind is more powerfully stirred by the anticipated immediate pleasure than by the thought of later suffering.

All of this is intensified when nervous balance has been weakened by exhaustion or when stimulants have smoothed the path for motor discharge.

If punishments are cruel, their severity brutalises and dulls the mind; if they are mild, their threat loses its force.

Worst of all, the fear of punishment vanishes entirely when the individual grows up in an atmosphere of crime—where the criminal is admired as a hero, where imprisonment is regarded as a commonplace inconvenience, no more remarkable than the other hardships of slum life; or where corruption, class injustice, reckless legislation, or public indifference to law deprives punishment of its emotional power as an inhibiting idea.

The more mechanical a system of punishment becomes, the more disappointing it proves. In this respect, the principle of probation represents genuine progress.

Far more important than fear are those formative influences that shape the inner life of the tempted individual: influences that diminish the emotional and motor force of forbidden desires, that regularly and vividly awaken social counter-ideas, that strengthen their inhibitory effect, and thereby weaken the primary impulse.

It must be said again, and without reservation: criminals are not born, but made—not even self-made, but made by others.

Society must therefore work negatively as well as positively. Negatively, it must remove those influences that operate in the opposite direction.

The atmosphere of criminality, the brutality and vulgarity, the meanness and frivolity that surround the developing mind must be eliminated.

If social contrasts are unavoidable and even productive of some good, the vulgar worship of mere wealth and the pitiless contempt for misery need not be tolerated. Above all, a sound mind can grow only in a well-treated body.

Far-sighted hygiene can prevent more crime than any statute. And this hygiene must extend far beyond the control of infectious disease or the sanitation of factories and tenements.

It must care no less for the overworked and misused senses and nervous systems—from the schoolroom to the stock exchange. There is no gain in avoiding epidemics of typhoid if we succumb to epidemics of mental breakdown. The entire rhythm of modern life undermines the instruments of nervous resistance, and the most immediate consequence is an increase in crime.

It is not the impulse itself that constitutes the criminal element, but the inability to resist the impulse. The banker who speculates with the funds of his institution is not criminal because such an idea arises in his mind, but because that idea is not checked by counter-ideas—and because society itself has helped to weaken the barriers that might have restrained the ruinous act.

Negative precautions, however, must be supplemented by positive ones. Hygiene must not merely remove what is harmful; it must actively build what is healthy. In the sphere of mental hygiene this principle is even more imperative.

To create a public life that offers example and inspiration to the humblest, that fills even the lowest with civic pride, would be the most effective way to abolish penitentiaries.

Public welfare must provide to every individual—through work, political participation, education, art, and religion—a sense of life-interest and life-content in which envy has no place. From this soil must grow the counter-ideas that automatically inhibit immoral impulses.

Yet no public system can replace the simplest and purest forces of human life: personal interest, sympathy, and direct human connection.

Everything that strengthens family life and resists its dissolution, everything that brings personal warmth to the isolated and abandoned, works toward the prevention of crime. How often a criminal career has been transformed simply because the fatal prejudice was abandoned—that prejudice which treats every criminal as a fundamentally different being—and because genuine sympathy, not patronising charity, was offered. To make a person feel recognised as an equal is to draw him back toward decency.

Those who study criminals psychologically know well that such recognition requires no condescension. They are the equals of the unpunished.

They may be dull, lazy, vehement, reckless, uneducated, unemotional, or egotistic—but all of these traits are found abundantly on the safe side of the legal boundary as well. Society readily bows to stupidity, laziness, recklessness, and egotism when circumstances have secured a sufficient balance. The inner self is not different; only the surroundings are. Bad example, overwhelming temptation, the saloon, the cruelty of misfortune may in a single reckless hour destroy that balance.

Here, finally, lies the profound significance of a true confession. The man who confesses places himself once more on equal ground with the honest majority.

He returns to the community of those who seek both justice and health. He renounces his identification with the criminal role and expels the crime from his life as one expels a foreign body. A genuine confession restores the fundamental unity of existence and offers the strongest safeguard against relapse.

The psychologist—though I speak with some hesitation, since observations in this field are still limited and the subject is new—may even be able, through experiment, to estimate whether a true confession is probable.

Every human action strives toward satisfaction, and satisfaction is impossible without inner unity.

Those who live wholly in the present find satisfaction in immediate experience; pleasure absorbs them completely, and unity of mind is achieved. Others live oriented toward the future; present suffering is overcome by hope, and unity arises from anticipation. Neither of these types is inclined toward liberating confession.

But it is different with those whose memory is vivid and active, whose minds constantly turn back to the past. In them there arises an enduring conflict between memories of purity, childhood, parental love, friendship, and faith, and the anxiety and misery of the present.

The craving for unity must end this struggle. Confession reconnects present and past and casts out the intrusive element of shame. Where psychological examination reveals such a living, vivid memory, the likelihood that a confession is genuine is high.

The criminal deed, in such cases, is almost a split-off fragment of consciousness, a dissociated part of the personality, and confession decisively severs it.

But when it is too late—when the split-off part has grown stronger, has become the dominant self—then prevention through social hygiene is nearly impossible. The professional criminal is, as a rule, lost. Society must then consider only how to protect itself from the harm he inflicts. Such a person must be removed from the commonwealth, just as the insane must be removed from the public arena of life. Short sentences for the professional criminal are useless and harmful in every respect. His career stands as a grim warning against postponing prevention until society—carelessly ignoring psychology—has itself manufactured the hopeless criminal.

The End

www.ingramcontent.com/pod-product-compliance
Lightning Source LLC
LaVergne TN
LVHW100731061126
851857LV00011B/487
* 9 7 8 9 3 7 7 0 7 8 4 8 5 *